am's Fillmore Auditorium

IE CREAM

(Clapton, Ginger Baker, & Jack Bruce)

Y • MARCH 7 & 10 AT THE FILLMORE

GEARY IN SAN FRANCISCO

Y MARCH 8 & 9 AT WINTERLAND

INER IN SAN FRANCISCO

WINTERLAND

$2.99 each

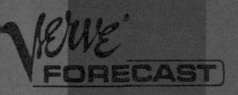

JAMES COTTON
$2.99

BLOOD,
SWEAT &
TEARS
$2.99

NEXT WEEK — BILL GRAHAM PRESENTS —

THURS. AT FILLMORE — TRAFFIC, LOVECRAFT, BLUE CHEER

FRIDAY AT WINTERLAND — TRAFFIC, LOVECRAFT, BLUE CHEER

CREAM

CLAPTON, BRUCE & BAKER
SITTING ON TOP OF THE WORLD

SAN FRANCISCO, FEBRUARY–MARCH
1968

Edoardo Genzolini

With Contributions by | Tony Palmer & Bill Halverson

SCHIFFER PUBLISHING

4880 Lower Valley Road • Atglen, PA 19310

Designed by Christopher Bower
Cover design by Christopher Bower
Type set in Glodok/Minion Pro

ISBN: 978-0-7643-6592-8
Printed in China

Published by Schiffer Publishing, Ltd.
4880 Lower Valley Road
Atglen, PA 19310
Phone: (610) 593-1777; Fax: (610) 593-2002
Email: Info@schifferbooks.com
Web: www.schifferbooks.com

For our complete selection of fine books on this and related subjects, please visit our website at www.schifferbooks.com. You may also write for a free catalog.

Schiffer Publishing's titles are available at special discounts for bulk purchases for sales promotions or premiums. Special editions, including personalized covers, corporate imprints, and excerpts, can be created in large quantities for special needs. For more information, contact the publisher.

We are always looking for people to write books on new and related subjects. If you have an idea for a book, please contact us at proposals@schifferbooks.com.

Front and back cover photos by Nick Schram

Endsheet photos from the *Berkeley Barb,* March 8, 1968

Eric Clapton's "The Fool" SG photos by John Peden

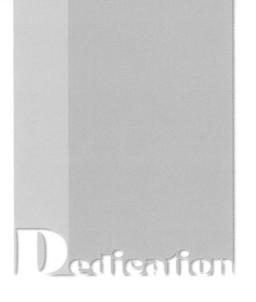

Dedication

To my music mates Luigi Gresele, Ruggero Fornari, Lorenzo Brilli, Niccolò Tommasini, and Emilio Seri . . . to our jazz and blues "ancient and modern" days.

Contents

This book comes from a long time ago. I will try to tell what I feel would be nice to know about its background, trying—at the same time—not to ramble too much. Sometimes, however, it is just inevitable, since some creations are so connected to life that it is just impossible not to end up trespassing other territories and talking about something else; after all, like Robert Henri wrote, "We value art not because of the skilled product, but because of its revelation of a life's experience." For this, I can only hope my readers will identify with what I will tell here.

This story dates back to a time in life that writer Paul Nizan won't let anyone say are the best years of your life—the teenage years. I doubt anyone would prove him wrong. However, the intensity of experiences witnessed at that age and their impact on a yet-fragmented self of a teenager is undeniable. As for me, what helped sublimate the emotional turbulence of those years and make me remember it today as somehow worth it was music from the sixties and the seventies.

My parents, Afra and Marco, are widely responsible for that. Music of Jackson Browne, Cat Stevens, Pink Floyd, King Crimson, and many artists more filled our house; records started playing one after another without me even noticing, to the extent that this music became part of my genetic code. For this reason, no matter how I tried, I couldn't and won't ever be able to grow out of it.

Luckily, that music wasn't just something I experienced in my domestic context, and that is what made it really special; out of synchronicity, I met friends with whom I could share my tastes.

In the infinite sea of insecurities during middle school, my classmate Sebastiano became my beacon. He was the first friend who could see through the facade of what I showed of myself. We were both precocious, in that we had interests that no one else around us had at our age. We loved cinema and had a cult for movies that, back in 2004, I bet none of our generation of 1991 even knew existed. I am sure we were the only ones back then in our city, and of the few in general, at thirteen/fourteen, to be hard-core fans of the original *Mad Max* trilogy long before it returned to fashion in 2015 through a new sequel.

We also loved to listen to Yvonne Elliman and KC and the Sunshine Band from the movie *Saturday Night Fever*. The tight fellowship between me and Sebastiano soon and spontaneously generated rituals that became sacred and long lasting, at least for those last two years at middle school, brief but so meaningful. Just like philosopher Andrea Emo said, "Rare are eternal moments in our life; eternity is temporary, but then the moment is eternal." Our rituals were definitely made of that.

These rituals consisted of Saturday nights we would spend watching specific movies until the break of dawn. Apart from the first two *Mad Max* titles, which often started our evenings, and *The Blues Brothers*, which ended our marathons on Sunday mornings, our favorites were seen in the middle of the night and were *American Graffiti* by George Lucas and *Fandango* by Kevin Reynolds; mainly, coming-of-age movies that must have been significant to us since we could feel and be self-aware of the changes we were going through as teenagers, at the speed of time.

Something in *Fandango* got me in particular the first time I saw it, and it was two songs that opened and closed the movie: "Badge," by Cream, and "Can't Find My Way Home," by Blind Faith. Although they were completely different songs, they had an intense melancholic feel conveyed particularly by what I later discovered was a common denominator—Eric Clapton's guitar. A fluid solo that couldn't be closer to an extremely expressive cry, in one song, while an intimate, comforting, embracing acoustic arpeggio, in the other. Those songs went straight to my soul, just like everything else I later discovered of Clapton, which, funnily enough, always happened through movies, particularly those by Martin Scorsese: the piano part in "Layla," heard in *Goodfellas*, but mostly, "Sunshine of Your Love," in the same movie, and "Stepping Out" in *Mean Streets*.

"That band Cream again. I must listen to more of them," I thought.

Meanwhile, time was running ahead quickly, and I was always going more backward with my listening, until I became hopelessly stuck in the sixties and in their kaleidoscopic net of expressions. This obsession went on until it generated three main paradigms of my tastes—two bands, the Who and Cream, and one place, San Francisco, which, in my mind, was synecdochically represented by two venues, the Fillmore Auditorium and Winterland, two very special venues that seemed to bring out the best, the essence, of the musicians who played there. I was so obsessed with these two venues that, in 2006, the MSN username I chose was "FillmoreGenzo"!

The Who and Cream are obviously very different. Yet, initially, both bands had an impact on me that was equally so strong that they struggled to coexist and fit together in the selective self of the fifteen-year-old I was. Very childishly, I couldn't accept being equally "loyal" and "committed" to both bands! As I grew up, I realized the Who and Cream had played two different roles in my life and blended equally harmonically in me.

The Who taught me spiritually; their music and Pete Townshend's lyrics were an unlimited source of strength, motivation, and self-esteem that shook my troubled and insecure self and made me react to problems. The best wish I could give to any teenager is to discover the Who at fifteen.

Cream, on the other hand, had the same strong impact, but musically. They taught me so much about music, from the sense of musicianship to that of improvisation. The best version of Cream I could relate to was the one live in 1968 at the Fillmore and Winterland.

Cream, San Francisco, and 1968 represented a perfect formula, which explains the necessity for me to make this book and to include "Sitting on Top of the World" in its subtitle. When I heard that song for the first time on *Wheels of Fire*, I couldn't help but picture Cream at the Fillmore and Winterland in early 1968. My mind went there automatically.

Just recently, when I discovered a never-heard-before tape I will talk about further on in this book, I realized that Cream even played that blues traditional at Winterland on March 9. That was quite a coincidence that made my choice even more meaningful.

Some might argue that such a title would have fit better for a book about Cream's first San Francisco experience in August–September 1967, since by the time Cream returned at the Fillmore in March 1968, they were described as a band that had already started to wear away, with a playing that had become self-indulgent and an image that was getting hypertrophic. Regardless of the fact that I don't share this vision, my choice for "Sitting on Top of the World" in the subtitle doesn't mean to convey or reflect a prejudice and my subjective point of view; it means to represent a fact and describe Cream's status by the time they returned to San Francisco in early 1968. They were objectively sitting on top of the world; either it was good or bad for them.

And, that aside, the music they played from March 7 to March 10 is extremely inspiring and has always been, since I first heard it.

I couldn't get tired of listening to Ginger Baker's drum solos, much to the complaints of my neighbors; Eric Clapton was and still is one of my favorite guitarists, in terms of tone and dynamics control, let alone his aesthetic magnetism onstage. Furthermore, the fluidity of his playing has always made me think of it as a perfect musical example of the notion of "Apollonian" as used by Friedrich Nietzsche in *The Birth of Tragedy*. In this book, the German philosopher deals with the Greek tragedy genre, describing its two main elements, Dionysian—lack of rationality and unbridled passion—and Apollonian—reason, harmony, and restraint. These latter attributes are ones I have always found in Eric Clapton's playing. Even when he is asked in his famous 1968 interview by BBC director Tony Palmer to give an example of aggression in his playing, Clapton seems to never lose control and focus.

Jack Bruce, however, was the one who shaped me the most musically. He was the bass player I looked up to as my main influence. I remember getting a red SG for my seventeenth birthday and making the first steps on it by jamming along with "Spoonful," exploring the fret board and trying to imitate Bruce's figures. I did the same with John Entwistle's, Phil Lesh's, and Felix Pappalardi's lines, but Jack Bruce was my main influence. This takes me up to 2009.

I am eighteen, I write for a local newspaper, I have been through two bands, and now I am making the queue to a concert with my keyboard player and music companion Luigi, "Gigi," with whom I have a progressive rock band called BMS, which stands for Blue Melted Steel. The sick reason for this choice is long lost to time. We all are excited, since we are waiting to get in to see no less than Jack Bruce with Robin Trower.

I am all geared up with video and photo cameras and the *Disraeli Gears* CD I bought two years before, hoping to sneak in at the end of the show to get it signed by Jack. I still regret not having brought anything of Procol Harum to get autographed by Trower.

At (almost) seventeen, in full Jack Bruce mood. *Photo by Edoardo Genzolini*

Nemo sleeping with my SG EB0. *Photo by Edoardo Genzolini*

At school, 2008. *Photo by Edoardo Genzolini*

The venue is a Roman amphitheater just outside our town of Perugia, and while we are all given numbered bleachers, Gigi and I boldly sit on the grass a few feet away from the stage and immediately tell the two security guards nearby that we are from the press. It was such a small, intimate context, with such a small audience, that no checks on our identity were made, and we were allowed to stay there for the show.

The two sixties veterans were promoting their new album *Seven Moons* and were accompanied by Gary Husband on the drums. Apart from three or four songs from the new release, of which I vividly remember the opening title track, the repertoire featured many Cream songs: "White Room," "Sunshine of Your Love," "Politician," and "We're Going Wrong" are those I remember, but there might have been more. I should check my video.

The concert is, to say the least, special, but the best part of that experience comes right after. Some of you may be familiar with Robert Fripp's "Jimi Hendrix story," from the first and very special time when the two guitarists met. Well, I would never put my name in the same text where Robert Fripp or Jimi Hendrix are mentioned, but what would unfold a few minutes after Jack Bruce and Robin Trower played the last note gave me, like Robert Fripp, a "famous musician story" to tell. That's right, I met Jack Bruce and was totally unprepared for it.

Given the modest audience and the intimacy of the context, an opportunity is given to anyone who wants to actually meet the musicians backstage. I immediately scoot toward Jack Bruce, dropping all my gear into Gigi's hands so he could immortalize the moment. I approach Bruce, trying to be discreet and calm, but the most undefined mix of feelings can't help pouring out of me, making me look exactly like I wish I never did in front of my bass mentor. As I frantically hand him the CD booklet to sign, I go, "Jack, I would like to thank you, since you are the reason why I am a bass player. I owe it all to you."

Jack Bruce live at Trasimeno Blues Festival (Perugia, Italy) on July 24, 2009. *Photo above by Edoardo Genzolini; photo below by Luigi Gresele*

He looks at me and, without waiting more than a second, replies, with that dry and unmistakable Scottish accent, "Oh, I am terribly sorry. Now, go get a job and get your hair cut!"

The way I reacted to his reply is an example of how never to act, not only in front of musicians of such caliber but in front of anyone; I burst out laughing and continuously thanked him for the autograph, then giving him my hand, hoping he could give me his to shake, but I got his elbow instead. So, we gave each other an "elbow kiss" just like Gene Wilder and Madeline Kahn in *Young Frankenstein*. "Taffeta, dear."

I feel obviously embarrassed about that episode, thinking of it now, but, at the same time, I acknowledge I couldn't have acted differently; I was just an eighteen-year-old guy meeting his idol for the first and, unfortunately, last time.

Dear Jack, wherever you may be now, I wanted to reassure you that I got a job, but my hair is still long.

Jack Bruce at Trasimeno Blues Festival (Umbria, Italy) on July 24, 2009. *Photo by Edoardo Genzolini*

Jack & Edoardo. Trasimeno Blues Festival, July 24, 2009. *Photo by Luigi Gresele*

Acknowledgments

The impulse that gave the long-nurtured idea of this book the definitive go-ahead comes from the long and stimulating conversations that took place in the last three years with three incredibly inspiring people: Michael Chaiken, Larry Yelen, and Christian Larsen. Michael and I first connected in 2019; I had found rare reel-to-reels containing unheard recordings of different bands made from the audience at Bill Graham's venues Fillmore, Winterland, and Fillmore West, including Cream's almost complete Winterland two-set show from March 9, 1968, of which one day I posted a brief excerpt of "Tales of Brave Ulysses" on Instagram. I was aware and was an assiduous and active follower of a profile named "clapton_was_god," which I looked upon as one of the quintessential embodiments of archival research, other than the epitome of Eric Clapton's iconography. I tagged that page on my video, hoping to rouse some interest. A few minutes later, I was already talking about music photography and archival research with the person behind that carrier of *trésors trouvés*, Michael Chaiken, who I later also discovered is curator of the Bob Dylan Archive in Tulsa, Oklahoma. The fruitful connection with Michael led to meeting Larry Yelen, archive producer / director of archival research for various Eric Clapton documentary projects, including *Eric Clapton: Life in 12 Bars* and *Eric Clapton: Nothing but the Blues*, and Christian Larsen, author of my favorite book ever on Eric Clapton, *Clapton Live History*, which embodies a conception of "labor of love" I can totally relate to.

I feel privileged and grateful that my recent years were positively influenced by the vibes of these three people. I hope the materials featured in this book can give them as much inspiration as I got from them. With equal importance, I would like to thank two more people I have known since the making of my Who book: Tony Palmer and Nick Schram. I find Tony's memories from the time he spent with Cream in San Francisco an extremely precious contribution to this book, just like all of Tony's works represent an essential and indispensable contribution to the understanding of cultural and societal aspects of specific times of our history.

Just like Tony, Nick Schram is an eye- and earwitness who should be protected by UNESCO; in a nutshell, from the little I have been privileged to know about his life, I would sum it up as "too much for one book or one movie." That might be a tagline, Nick, in case you will make up your mind about telling the world about your crazy, incredible, inspiring life through a movie or a book, my friend. Your stories and the tapes you made, to which I have had access to, represent the essential yet never-before-sung melody of the polyphony that was the sixties.

Thanks to Pat Thomas for making the connection with Bill Halverson possible, and thanks to Bill for disclosing exclusive and fascinating facts from his recording experience with Cream.

Many thanks also to Paul Bonick for his photos and for his great generosity. A warm thank you to all those who took part in this work, whose names can be found throughout the text.

To Be Where
I'm Going

"The prototype for a whole new thing" . . . the "simultaneous dissolution of every molecule in existence" . . . the "blending of old into new and new into newer, testing, withdrawing, or lunging ahead" . . .

"Simply, the end of the universe. Or maybe the creation of one."[1]

When Cream formed, in June 1966, no one knew what they were. The press seemed trapped in a conceptual cul de sac, constantly bringing up definitions that made newspaper articles almost look like surrealistic *feuilletons*. Journalists and music critics seemed caught up in an almost intellectual exercise consisting of coming up with the most-creative definitions for the new three-piece band formed by the "cream of the crop" of the surrounding music scene: Ginger Baker, Jack Bruce, and Eric Clapton.

Everything was being said about Cream, except what they really were. They simply seemed to be impervious to every attempt at classification. They were indeed aware of the confusion and excitement around them, but they didn't seem to care about doing anything in order to avoid it, and they carelessly led popular opinion anywhere they wanted, starting from the image they created that everybody struggled to define—Clapton:

I had a concept, yeah. It was a throw-over of my art school scene, something like Dada. The Cream was originally going to be a stage presentation as well as the music, like happenings on stage. We did one gig, the first one we did, and we had a gorilla on stage, a stuffed one. And we had a lot of strange little things happening like this and it didn't work, nothing happened 'cause we were so involved in music that we just forgot about all these things.[2]

Back then, Eric couldn't know that within a short time, by the wake of Cream, his band would have revealed exactly what lay behind the concept he used in this interview, "happenings on stage." By this expression, Eric surely had in mind something more visual, but after some time he might have realized that Cream, by its very nature, had been a "happening" in the sense of an "event": something far from the concept of reproducibility (with which, inevitably, Cream had to confront themselves, through their live recordings); also something far from the sense of predictability, to the extent that every event itself, just like every performance of Cream, is a *unicum* and thus always different; also something that—again *necessarily*, as an event, by its very nature—has to deal with the sense of limit and of ending.

History would have taught that Cream's destiny was an exact reflection of that *thing* they played, which, like we said, no one managed to define; they *were* what they played, and at the end, they couldn't have proved truer to their nature.

The press wasn't the only one disoriented: at the time when Cream broke into a music scene that looked totally unprepared for them, neither did they know where this road would lead. They knew only that they had to be together.

When Eric Clapton, Jack Bruce, and Ginger Baker teamed up, it happened out of necessity, and, like happens with necessity, they couldn't wait for collective comprehension to manifest themselves. What they had to say was urgent, and immediate.

"We had no other interest," remembered Eric. "There was nothing else going on. There was no family, there was no desire for success, there was no commerciality involved, there was no responsibility other than that unique moment in time when we were together. And for a short sweet period of time it was unfettered, extreme, and beautiful."[3]

While most of the press was all uptight about how hard it was to write about Cream—about how they were "totally eclectic," how their records "show strains of almost every musical form imaginable," how "they just go and go, more like a symphony, without repeating themselves"[4]—what seems unquestionable, as *G.Q. Scene* reads, is that Cream were "three musicians playing three musics. Three musics that make a larger music."[5]

These three musicians agreed with the fact that what they were doing was unique, a mixture of different styles each of the trio brought with him into the group: "Our music cannot be categorized because a lot of the material we play is not blues; it's another thing completely, probably brand new," said Eric to *Boston Sunday Globe* in early 1968.[6]

The powerful chemistry that brought the three musicians together was the result of the contamination of three different backgrounds and a common attitude toward music that was extremely professional, almost sacred and pure.

Eric Clapton was and still is a blues purist; yet, he was described at the time as "so far away from clichés that he played things you've never heard before," as *Hit Parader* wrote in 1968.[7] Eric Clapton had gained the reputation of "God" for being looked up to as the finest guitarist in London. His dedication to the instrument was all-embracing, with a perfectionism that while offstage almost resulted in hermitage, onstage, it manifested through an ecstatic, cathartic immobility and focus. He was so restless to reflect to the exterior the changes he was going through: his music skills would evolve along with his aesthetic look—like a chameleon, he was ever changing and fleeing. Before joining Cream, Eric had made himself popular in the British scene by serving as lead guitarist of blues bands such as the Yardbirds and John Mayall's Bluesbreakers, which he left not long after he joined them, driven by such an ambition and vision for his music that made him perceive the surrounding offer as unsatisfactory.

Jack Bruce had classical education and was proficient in piano, double bass, and cello. He studied at the Royal Scottish Academy of Music but soon dropped out when he became aware of the incompatibility between his vocations and the conservative, narrow-minded structure of that institution. Bruce was also a trad and modern jazz enthusiast just like his historical music pal and nemesis Ginger Baker, whose drumming, apart from jazz, was also deeply rooted in African rhythms, to which he was introduced by his mentor, drummer Phil Seamen. Together, Bruce and Baker had created the rhythmic backbone of an extremely inspiring alternative to the more diffuse and blasé rock-and-roll scene in London, an alternative represented by guitarist Alexis Korner with his Blues Incorporated.

More than a band, Blues Incorporated was much rather a "concept," given the fluid lineup that saw musicians coming and going. Among these were harmonica player Cyril Davies, singer Long John Baldry, saxophonist Dick Heckstall-Smith, piano player Graham Bond, drummer Charlie Watts (who was replaced by Ginger Baker), and Jack Bruce. Blues Incorporated was the first successful collective to play R & B in the UK, which, thanks to Alexis Korner and the R 'n' B Nights he held at the Ealing Club, in West London, helped spread an enthusiasm for the genre, attract musicians, and inspire them to play together. This process contributed to bringing Charlie Watts and Mick Jagger together, as well as Jack Bruce, Ginger Baker, Dick Heckstall-Smith, and Graham Bond, who would soon all leave Blues Incorporated to form the Graham Bond Organisation.

The Organisation was welcomed as an exciting jazz and R & B band, but its first lineup didn't last long, since Bruce and Baker parted ways because of the respective musical personalities and inclinations, which were so strong, well defined and extremely self-aware that they wound up clashing most of the time. Before his short experience with Manfred Mann, Jack Bruce went to play for an equally short time in the Bluesbreakers. It was there that he and Clapton met and became aware of their respective talents.

Ginger Baker soon realized that his and Jack Bruce's destiny couldn't be divided that simply: when Ginger invited Eric Clapton to form a band, after hearing him play with the Bluesbreakers in Oxford in May 1966, the guitarist immediately agreed, the only condition being that Jack Bruce could join as a third member. However begrudgingly, Baker accepted. This intolerance was cast aside, albeit momentarily.

Cream were formed by three musicians individually dissatisfied with the surrounding context, who found themselves drawn to one another by the same condition and by the pure and simple aim to play and make music. Their way.

"They had no idea what it would sound like," wrote *Hit Parader* in 1968. "When we first formed, we had all just discovered ourselves completely, musically. We had a vague idea of what we'd each sound like but we didn't know what the combination would be," said Eric. "We had to try. And it worked." "We all just played what we felt," added Ginger.

"You can't call it blues," continues Eric. "You might catch a little of it in my playing, but as a unit, it's just our music."[8]

What we gather is that Cream was an instinctual impulse, a spontaneous manifestation of being that couldn't be further from being determined or classified, which, yet, came into a music world ruled by the cultural industry principles of categorization and rationalization through charts and their disposable, fleeting implications.

If, on one hand, management could mean a necessity, in that it could help the band gain recognition, on the other hand, it put Cream in front of compromises that affected their expression.

The introduction of Reaction Label manager Robert Stigwood was a decision wanted by Ginger Baker; Stigwood had managed the Graham Bond Organisation, and, according to Ginger, he could help Cream pull off. But when the band's first single, "Wrapping Paper," came out, it wasn't what everyone was expecting from such an unbridled band with such a heterogeneous lineup. It was clearly a Robert Stigwood operation aimed for the Top 20. This episode introduced the struggle that Cream suffered from the start of finding themselves: between trying to live up to and to keep up with a pop image wanted by their management, with a defined and money-aimed studio and live schedule, and preserving their own creative nature and ideals that brought them together so spontaneously. In time, however, Cream would have gained intellectual autonomy and control as a studio band and would have presented themselves onstage in a totally different outfit than in the studio, creating an intriguing and original dichotomy.

But back in mid-1966, when Cream started off, everything was still different, and the context was not helping either: "The British scene is so small. Everybody knows what everyone else is doing and the whole thing thrives on competition," observed Eric.[9]

England proved a context far from fitting for the both purist and avant-gardist attitude pursued by Cream. The three musicians' playing was a maelstrom of influences that was grounded deeply in the tradition of American blues, jazz, and improvisation, something that didn't get through the British scene the way Cream hoped. "In England there aren't any roots," said Eric. "There are less [sic] people interested in music because they don't have the culture or the money."[10] Jack Bruce attributed it to the fact that "the Europeans have had second-hand experiences through records and cover groups."[11] More than music itself, more than musicianship and playing music, what seemed to be more important in England was the fashion side of it; the superficial implication that made one band valid for then being forgotten after a short time. "Instead of fifteen minutes of fame, you only get three minutes. So everything gets forgotten and traditions don't get passed on," remembered Pete Brown, co-lyricist of some Cream songs.[12]

Cream felt they had to go where their music was born to finally be able to express themselves freely and without compromises; without having to justify their choices or adjust their potential for a hardly receptive public.

The year 1967, paraphrasing the Zombies, "would be their year": in April, with the first album *Fresh Cream* released in late 1966, Cream set off for the conquest of America.

"*Fresh Cream* had been released in America on the Atco label (Atlantic Records subsidiary), and it had gotten into the lower reaches of the US album chart," said Ginger. "It only went in at number 198, but it was *there*. The way was open for the band to start its conquest of the West."[13]

And You Touch the Distant Beaches, 1967

America is the place that changed Cream forever, collectively and individually, for the better and worse. The States showed the three musicians "the most potential good . . . and the most potential evil,"[1] said Eric, looking back on the band's career in November 1968, a later yet not-so-distant time. But mostly, still an unpredictable time, when Cream arrived in the United States for the first time a year before and was amazed at how different things were from every other place.

"It was the beginning of a disenchantment with England," said Eric, "where it seemed there wasn't really room for more than one person to be popular at a time. What I loved about America was that it seemed such a broad breeding ground for different acts and talents, and different forms of music. . . . There seemed to be room for anyone to make a living out of it and be at the forefront of what they were doing."[2]

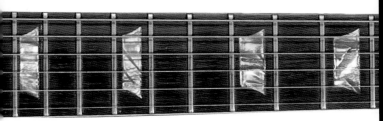

The first stop was in New York and consisted of a series of appearances at the RKO Theater for Murray the K's "Music in the 5th Dimension" shows. The format, created by the DJ who contributed to the popularity of the Beatles and the Rolling Stones in America, turned out to be a grueling commitment of five shows a day, with each show lasting only around five minutes, for ten days. This whirlwind saw Cream sharing the bill with other bands and artists, including another new act from England that, like Eric, Jack, and Ginger, had just arrived in the US—the Who. This context made Cream perform way below their potential, leaving them room to play continually and mechanically—according to Eric—only one song off their *Fresh Cream* album, "I Feel Free."[3] They didn't, in fact.

The brief New York experience proved disappointing, and the band got out of it bitter and exhausted: "The whole thing had nothing to do with music," said Eric to *Melody Maker*, "nothing whatsoever. We took the actual show as a joke."[4]

New York, however, would turn out as but a false start. A misleading prelude. It would not be long before Cream's impression of the New World would change radically and better than they could have imagined before.

Fillmore Auditorium. August 22–September 3, 1967. *Photograph by Frank Zinn / courtesy of Rich Martin Frost*

With the start of the first proper US tour, the destiny of Cream started to be fulfilled.

It was on a Tuesday, August 22, 1967, that Cream arrived in San Francisco and played in a venue that the band would soon be directly associated with, almost becoming synonymous: the Fillmore Auditorium. The Fillmore immediately felt like the first context in which Cream could freely express themselves, with no compromise. It was more than that: it gave them the inputs that they still didn't know they needed to become what they wanted. "The first time I went to San Francisco," remembers Eric, "I experienced the kind of more introverted or serious or introspective attitude toward our music. . . . I was encouraged really to get outside of the format. I was encouraged to experiment."[5]

Fillmore Auditorium. August 22–September 3, 1967. *Courtesy of Stephen L. Grimm*

Jack remembers that "the first night we played at the Fillmore our music changed, really took a jump ahead. The audiences here are great." "They're a completely new thing," Eric concurs. "They seem to have the same attitude toward music as the musician himself. There was very much a whole kind of Fillmore energy coming off the audience that combined with the band."[6]

All of a sudden, discovering the Fillmore and San Francisco made the necessity for a definition for Cream's music pointless: as the band started playing, the place responded. Music was what it was all about.

San Francisco proved the perfect context for a "thing" like Cream, and the Fillmore became the place that mirrored the vision and ethics behind the band's attitude. In a way, for Cream, the Fillmore became eponymous for America: "There was a time when you wanted to make America your home," observed *Beat Instrumental*. "What are your feelings now that you have seen it?" "I'd still like to live there," said Eric. "I've discovered from recent visits that if you are involved in music then this is your home. I suddenly had the feeling that I'd been away from home and had just returned. If I did stay there, I'd like to live on the West Coast. On the West Coast there's a very creative atmosphere. It's very encouraging. It's inspiring. In New York you've just got to work or you'll lose your mind; it's so neurotic."[7]

The Fillmore and San Francisco would give the three musicians an overview of the American music scene and the ethics and vision behind it: "American audiences are tired of going to listen to music and getting patches of personalities. Music can be a whole lot more than a Murray the K's ego trip."[8]

One of the elements largely responsible for the receptiveness of the scene was the man behind the Fillmore, Bill Graham. Born Wolfgang Volodja Grajonca, Bill was a Russian German Jew who escaped as a child the Nazis' spread in Europe. His long and strenuous escape finally ended when he got to New York at the age of eleven, after traveling from Germany through France, Spain, Portugal, Morocco, and Senegal. Bill grew up in the Bronx, where he cut his teeth and developed the street attitude that would later make him so recognizable. He first visited the Bay Area after discovering that one of his sisters, Rita, survived like him and was living in San Francisco. There, Bill found a quiet, heterogeneous, and inclusive city that "had a long tradition of embracing the unconventional."[9] Bill blended in by joining the Mime Troupe, hoping to finally have a way as an actor, a vocation that before arriving in San Francisco had taken him across America, between New York and Los Angeles.

The businessy attitude that he would have been mostly associated with started to slowly come out when he began to act less and started managing the troupe. "I seemed to have a knack for it," he acknowledged.[10]

This simple and apparently unimportant shift exemplifies the operation that would be led by Bill inside the San Francisco scene within a short time from then: taking over and managing something still in its embryonic, spontaneous form. What initially involved no money and blossomed as something antiestablishment, a new art form with new venues where it was being exhibited, soon started to grow a business around it through Bill. He had foresight.

Bill Graham's settling at the Fillmore in 1966 was the result of a monopoly operation led by him against his competitor in the San Francisco scene—Chet Helms and his Family Dog productions.

The Family Dog was a collective against which Bill started to go head to head since early November 1965. At that time, Mime Troupe member Ronald Davis had been arrested for obscenity while performing the Italian play *The Candle Bearer* by Giordano Bruno in Lafayette Park. Bill organized a party in the troupe's loft, with the intent to raise money for the collective's defense. What is emblematic, as Chet Helms remembered, is that Bill purposely organized the event aware of the dances that were going on the same night, organized by the Family Dog across town, at Longshoremen's Hall.[11]

Bill's tough, street attitude was immediately clear to the mellow, laid-back promoter Chet Helms.

After proving to be a surprisingly successful experience, with an unexpected and unprecedented attendance, Bill and the Mime Troupe went looking for a more suitable venue to hold other benefits, "for continued artistic freedom in the parks." *San Francisco Chronicle* journalist Ralph J. Gleason suggested the "Old" Fillmore Auditorium on Geary Boulevard. After two more Mime Troupe benefits held at the Fillmore in early 1966, Bill and Chet Helms even promoted a few dances together there, but Bill's dominant attitude would soon prevail.

After leaving the troupe, within a few months Bill got rid of Chet, too, and started running the Fillmore on his own. The last show the two promoters produced together was on April 9, 1966. Helms eventually took his production over to the Avalon Ballroom, on Sutter Street.

It is evident that Bill didn't create a scene; he helped it become self-aware and made it express its potential at its best. The Fillmore became the place in which such a purpose would be served.

The Fillmore, after its many incarnations as Majestic Hall and Academy of Music in the 1910s and as a jazz venue in the 1950s, became with Bill Graham the epicenter of a sociocultural shift in the way music would be performed by musicians and experienced by their audiences. Bill became aware of a spontaneous phenomenon that had been building up since the Acid Tests, a series of LSD-fueled parties held by author Ken Kesey and his group of wackos, named the Merry Pranksters, in La Honda in 1965, in which the San Francisco band the Warlocks, the embryonic stage of the Grateful Dead, used to play largely improvised sets. LSD would become illegal only the following year, but by the time of the Acid Tests, it had become the key to a new level of perception that leveled the boundaries of the mind and led to a deeper consciousness. This was due to Augustus Owsley Stanley III, who is responsible for distributing apparently three hundred thousand doses of acid in San Francisco after producing it privately in his place in Los Angeles between March and May 1965.[12]

From informal and unannounced happenings, the Acid Tests would be taken around California, leading the experience they offered to reach its climax with the Trips Festival at Longshoremen's Hall in San Francisco in January 1966.

Everything took a definitive turn when the acid edge of such a phenomenon met with Bill's rationality. He witnessed the atmosphere and formalized the formula. He made it "official"; he made it a standard. He brought that atmosphere to the Fillmore (the posters advertising Bill's dances at the Fillmore, in February 1966, even carried the wording "With Sights and Sounds of the Trips Festival"), from where it would reverberate through the American sociocultural fabric. A format was created.

At the Fillmore, people would dance to extremely heterogeneous lineups, with apparently incompatible and conflicting acts that wouldn't have shared the same stage anywhere else: the Who with Cannonball Adderley, the Velvet Underground & Nico with the Mothers of Invention (who would also open for Lenny Bruce on a later date), Big Mama Thornton with Paul Butterfield and Jefferson Airplane, Otis Redding with the Grateful Dead, Tim Buckley and the Chambers Brothers, and the list goes on.

By the tension that arose through that contamination, Bill would surreptitiously "educate" the audiences; either dancing or sitting down, people would listen to whoever was playing, thus contributing to generating mutual feedback between the artists and the audience. This made every night at the Fillmore a happening. For that and many other reasons, artists would rate the Fillmore as their best performance, and audiences still preserve cherished memories, albeit hazy, of those nights.

Bill couldn't have imagined he was preparing the field for what would become the show business world we know today, but whatever it would have become, its first incarnation couldn't have looked greater.

Cream's performances in those two weeks of August and September 1967 made no exception. Those nights were pure Fillmore experience:

> We were told by Bill that we could play anything we liked for as long as we liked, even if this meant us playing till dawn, and this is where we started openly exploring stuff. Anywhere else, we would probably have been a lot more concerned about presentation, but playing in the Fillmore, we soon realized that no one could see us because they were projecting light shows on to the band, so that we were actually in the light show. It was very liberating. We could just play our hearts out, without inhibition. . . . They were *listening*, and that encouraged us to go places we'd never been before. We started doing extended solos and were soon playing fewer and fewer songs but for much longer . . . I had never experienced anything like it. It was nothing to do with lyrics or ideas; it was much deeper, something purely musical. We were at our peak during that period.[13]

Fillmore Auditorium. August 22–September 3, 1967. *Photo by John Peden*

It is also important to point out that Bill Graham was the first person to treat Cream with the professionalism and concern they deserved. The tragic aspect about Cream's history lies in an incredible potential handled by shortsighted, unimaginative people, as Jack Bruce remembered:[14] "Our reputation only began to grow after we played at the Fillmore."[15] Before then, Cream had played only small, one-off, forty-five-minute shows in small venues, even missing the Monterey Pop Festival in June 1967, which would undoubtedly have given Cream a definitive go in the States before it actually happened. They had to wait for the end of the "Summer of Love" and play the Fillmore to make that "jump." Bill Graham seemed to be the only person who really saw the potential and who invested thoughtfully in the band by booking them not for one but for two weeks at his venue. Having the band onstage for this long would have allowed it to emerge and manifest for what it really was. He was the first one to valorize them.

Fillmore Auditorium. August 22–September 3, 1967. Paul Butterfield jams with Cream in the bottom photo. *Photos by John Peden*

Fillmore Auditorium. August 22–September 3, 1967. *Photos by John Peden*

Fillmore Auditorium. August 22–September 3, 1967. *Photo by John Peden*

Eric playing Harvey Mandel's tobacco Gibson ES335 at the Fillmore, by Paul Sommer

One of the first Cream shows I went to was somewhere during the week of August 22 - 27, 1967 at the old (original) Fillmore Auditorium on Geary Blvd in San Francisco. The opening act was Charlie Musslewhite's Southside Sound System, while the headliner was the Paul Butterfield Blues Band. Cream was second billed and went on before Butterfield.

Mike Bloomfield, who was the lead guitarist in the original Butterfield Band, had just left the group to start his own band, The Electric Flag. Elvin Bishop then stepped up to be the lead guitarist as is featured on their next record *The Resurrection of Pigboy Crabshaw* album that came out that year.

Guitar tech Burt Schrader helping Eric switch Harvey Mandel's 335 with the "Fool" SG. *Photo by John Peden*

The Southside Sound System was harmonica king Charlie Musslewhite's band, also from Chicago (like Butterfield). The lead guitar player in Charlie's band was Harvey Mandel who was playing a Fender Deluxe Reverb amp, miked into a Fender Dual Showman, placed on the other side of the stage.

During one of Cream's two sets was a tune that featured each player, solo, where the rest of the band dropped out. Ginger Bakers' tune was "Toad" that featured an extended drum solo. Eric Clapton's tune was "Steppin' Out." Eric was playing his painted Gibson SG (nicknamed "The Fool" that he got earlier that year).

During Clapton's solo, after the band dropped out, Eric broke his high "E" string. He kept playing. I thought it was Eric's guitar tech team came out on stage with Harvey Mandel's Gibson ES335 and put it on Eric while he was still playing his solo. They plugged the 335 into one of his two Marshall stacks and mid-phrase Eric switched to Harvey's guitar. Eric's road crew took his SG off stage to replace the E string. All this time Eric was soloing without Jack Bruce or Ginger Baker. From John Peden's photo, it looks like someone from Charlie Musslewhite's band, not a Cream tech or one of Bill Graham's guys, brought back Eric's SG, slipped it on and plugged it in. Still soloing, Eric switched back to his own SG and continued the solo. It took me a few moments to notice that his new string was not up to pitch but Eric played on it, tuned it up a little, played on it some more and then finished tuning it up . . . all while playing his "Steppin' Out" solo. I will never forget it.

Each band played two sets at the Fillmore, always. There were no seats (except a few rows of folding chairs near the front of the stage). Everyone sat on the floor in front of the chairs or stood. I was sitting right in front of Eric. During Cream's second set Eric invited Paul Butterflied to sit in with them. Hearing the best harmonica player alive play the blues with Cream was unforgettable. After Paul left the stage, Eric said, "I will be back to join Paul for their second set." Paul Butterfield went on for their second set at close to 1:00 a.m. They played and played and played. We were all waiting for Eric to join the band. My friend who drove that night said to me, "Paul . . . it is 4:00 a.m. and I am going home," "If you want a ride we need to go." Butterfield's band was still playing when we left and I don't know if Eric ever showed.

But where did all this success of Cream at the Fillmore really come from? Eric Clapton couldn't believe the reception they got from the San Francisco audience: "I didn't imagine that we'd be this popular, or that we'd be accepted as readily as we were," he said.[16] Everyone who saw them at the Fillmore reports to have witnessed something life-changing. Musicians who were in the audience changed their attitude after seeing Cream perform on those nights, as Jack Casady of Jefferson Airplane recalled: "Everybody got louder and harder and tougher after that."[17] It probably had to do with the fact that Cream had "brought it all back home"—an English band showing so much rooted familiarity with the blues must have made quite an impression on American audiences that found themselves watching "their" thing being played with such a drive and intensity— by only *three* musicians. Hearing local San Francisco bands play, Clapton wondered if their audiences had any knowledge of the blues, and he initially thought that many people were listening to this kind of repertoire for the first time through Cream. In fact, it wasn't really like that, but the jug band / country and folk influences among Bay Area bands were so rooted that it made their playing more mellow. While this was the case with bands such as the Grateful Dead or the Jefferson Airplane, it didn't apply, however, to all San Francisco bands, and Moby Grape was definitely more to Cream's liking.

The audience, treated to the hot-blooded professionalism of Cream, something they developed through playing the harsh and ramified UK club circuit, witnessed something epiphanic and gave the definitive feedback to the band that made them never look back to England.

Cream continued their first US tour playing the Whisky A Go Go in Los Angeles, the Psychedelic Supermarket in Boston, and the Action House on Long Island, New York, with their last dates at the Grande Ballroom in Detroit in mid-October, but those two weeks at the Fillmore Auditorium remained unsurpassed: "I haven't recovered from San Francisco yet," remembered Ginger when Cream returned to England later that year. "We really had a ball."[18]

29

Freaking out at the Fillmore

GEORGE ALMOND

We heard the Fillmore Auditorium, San Francisco, long before we reached it. It sounded like a huge bee jumping around the stretched parchment of a drum, the vibrations being squeezed through the square open windows of the building out into the warm Pacific air. Loitering, malingering and listening at the entrance of the large block building was the usual collection of hippies, destitutes and gutter-squatting individuals. For them, at least, the music and the message it carried was free. It cost us three dollars each to see the musicians at their posts.

A long-haired, square-spectacled mendicant came up to us at the kiosk. "Can you buy me a ticket, please? My friends inside will pay you back." Gullible, but aware of it, we bought him a ticket to the great annoyance of the beefy throw-out men, and he led us up the stairs into the darkness and promptly disappeared from our sight.

There were about 2,000 people in the building, some cross-legged on the floor, some dancing madly like blue ghosts in the infra-violet light and some, like us, just gaping at the spectacle. There were all sorts. Many were well-dressed college students with their dates, eager for a new-style entertainment. Then there were the groovy fired fellows, the hippies—beads, hats, beards and whiskers—all strolling about like miniature Rasputins, quite ignorant of the stares of the sightseers, who stood out easily in their dinner-jackets and police uniforms.

But we were all there for the spectacle and the spectacle presided with an overwhelming amount of self-assertion. We moved in an atmosphere, consisting of solid sound, which flooded from nine mansize loudspeakers on the stage. Slicing through the supercharged decibels of this medium were shafts of light from projectors on the balcony. They swept out like spokes of a fan to form multiple compositions and pictures on the screen above the group. Occasionally visible in this flickering kaleidoscope they played their instruments as if, and because, their lives depended on it. It was a group called the American Flag, clustered under the Stars and Stripes flying in an artificial breeze, that held the Auditorium on the end of its guitar picks and drum sticks. Sweating with the effort, the patriots bent their beards over their guitars and thrummed to the rhythm of their drummer who looked like Kenyatta's henchman with his hair flaring high towards the splurging oil projection on the screen behind him. The organist looked like a walrus wearing a cloth cap and his instrument, though tiny on the stage, made more noise than the biggest church organ in the world. We were all impressed.

But we could hardly fail to be impressed in some way, for the purpose of the music was to create a total preoccupation, which leaves no room nor desire for conversation. The volume shook the floorboards and the swelling acoustics were transformed into visual rhythm, by way of the oil projection with its chameleon qualities. All the spectacular effects were created by a bunch of ardent scraggy technicians huddling over their projectors, whirling coloured wheels, rapid-fire slide magazines and movie projectors, as if they were the very beginning of creation. On the left hand screen there were movie shorts of a policeman methodically and bestially banging his baton against his hand. He was replaced at times by hospitalised patients or preachers smiling sweetly and earnestly over the auditorium. This was the sick screen. On the other screens there was a mixture of ideas and patterns—a monkey changing into a beautiful girl model and then back again, flags and nudes, Nazis and flowers—all constantly changing their role and possible meaning. And in the middle, dominating the group, the hypnotic oil pattern that was small one moment, gigantic the next. It was just like a jellyfish having orgasm in a rainbow.

Eventually the American Flag wilted into silence and the crowd rested for a few minutes, preparing itself for the most fantastic, psychedelic, stimulating event of the evening. We were able to talk for a little while, though the ringing of music in our ears made hard work of this unnatural action. Once in the distance we glimpsed the golliwog head of our self-invited guest, but we had given up the idea of seeing our three dollars from him. We looked back to the stage. The stars of the evening, the big Fillmore Magnetism, were an English group, the Cream, which consisted of three musicians of outstanding quality. This we did not know, of course, when we joined those on the floor who were squatting patiently as the electricians shackled the volume boosters to the Cream's instruments. The audience hushed in anticipation of deep experience as the Cream trickled on to the stage in bright shirts and piped clashing pants. The gods were there and as the first number exploded into the auditorium, it was as though we were witnessing the explosion of a musical megaton bomb.

For nearly an hour the message of 1967 roared out, everyone interpreting it in their own way. For many of the Haight Ashbury league this was a musical thrill of rare vintage, whilst for the unenlightened there was a genuine respect for the abilities and talent of the Cream who were undisputed masters of their art. In solos of great length and complexity the guitar, the mouth-organ and the drums were treated to efforts so prodigious that we felt the Cream had gymnastic training for eight hours a day. The projection maestros rose also to the occasion, and with simulated lighting and voltage sparks, played a fire over the performers which burnt into the souls of the audience. It burned so much that, when at last the Cream retired from the stage, there could have been no one who had not felt some message from a realm beyond normal understanding . . .

Yes, we saw a lot that evening, and felt, without any help from any drugs, something of the power of the music, heaven or refuge. This was the intangible, a memory we could take home and think about. But there was something else we took home that night. It was the memory of a square-spectacled, long-haired hippie who ran up to us as we left the auditorium brandishing three dollar bills which he forced upon us with profuse thanks for the evening of his lifetime. ∎

Music Maker, February 1968

Eric Clapton's "The Fool" Gibson SG story, by John Peden

So what's the deal with this unique decorated guitar Eric Clapton is playing at the Fillmore Auditorium in 1967? It begins with a used 1964 Gibson SG Standard guitar acquired in London in 1967. Clapton under the spell of The Kings (Freddie, Albert and B.B.) had favored Gibsons with humbucking pickups already. He had played a red '64 335 and a 1960 Les Paul Standard famously with John Mayall's Bluesbreakers. Robert Stigwood, the manager that put Cream together, commissioned the Dutch design team "The Fool" consisting of Jose Leeger, Simon Koger and Marijke Posthuma to create a unified visual for Cream's equipment and stage costumes. The Fool was the hottest design team in fashion obsessed London at the time. They painted a multistory mural for the Beatles Baker St. shop, the Saville Theatre interiors and concert

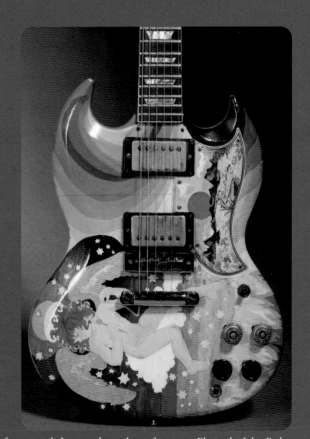

The state of the "Fool" guitar when it was bought in an online auction, after several changes throughout the years. *Photos by John Peden*

posters. For Cream they designed the stage clothes, Ginger Baker's bass drum head and most famously Clapton's SG Standard guitar. The guitar's stock tremolo was removed, a stop tailpiece was substituted and as was customary at the time Grover Rotomatic tuners replaced the original Klusons. Most assuredly control knobs came and went over time. It would be a waste of time and ink to describe the guitar you have only to look at the photos front and back. Similarly, you don't need my description of the music they produced. I will report that the extended solos that all members of Cream produced stunned and produced rapt attention from the audience. Cream transformed the Fillmore Auditorium alternately into an intimate jazz club or a majestic concert hall.

Mike Bloomfield early on had become a musical talent scout for Bill Graham advising him as to which acts to book. When Cream was originally booked, they were to share the stage with the Butterfield Blues Band with Mike Bloomfield on lead guitar. Unfortunately, Mr. Bloomfield left Butterfield the week before these gigs to start his own band, The Electric Flag which was also booked as the third act on the bill. However, Bloomfield was unable to play the shows, so a little-known band from Michigan, the Prime Movers, was substituted on at least one night. Butterfield recruited Harvey Mandel to take Bloomfield's position in his band. I believe it is Mandel's tobacco 335 that Clapton used when "The Fool" needed tuning or he tired of it.

The state of the "Fool" guitar when it was bought in an online auction, after several changes throughout the years. *Photos by John Peden*

Mike Bloomfield perhaps is the only guitarist at that time who could have stood toe to toe with Clapton on that stage. One can only imagine.

Cream's performances transformed the audience and the Fillmore's reputation as an institution that expected the highest musical standards from its performers. Note how many musicians choose to record "Live at The Fillmore" LPs there.

For this write-up, John Peden would like to credit Keith Williams/"five watt world" YouTube channel ("The Guitars of Eric Clapton: A Short History"), and J. Craig Oxman, "Clapton's Fool: History's greatest guitar?," *Vintage Guitar Magazine*, 2011.

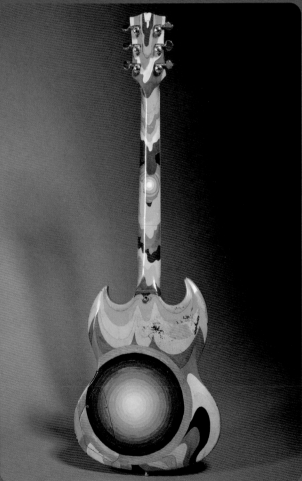

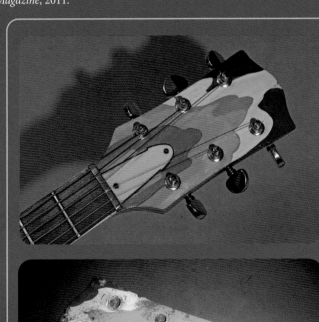

The rebuilt and the original headstock. *Photos by John Peden*

At the Marquee (London) in early 1968, before departing for the United States. *All photos by Chris Thomas*

3 Standing at the Crossroads, 1968

Madison Square Garden, New York. November 2, 1968. *Photo by Sunny Paul*

"I dream of the day where there will be no more categories. There will just be live music and recorded music. People won't have to live up to a style any more. Music will just be people playing what they want. That's where I want to go."

This is what Eric said to *Hit Parader* in late 1967.[1] A year later, in 1968, we would discover that the direction Eric said he wanted to take his music, and Cream, would lead to the West. The scene would be San Francisco again.

This traces back to the band's natural and most essential trait: Jack Bruce had said that Cream was like two bands—a studio band, where experimentation would emerge through complex arrangements, and a live band, where experimentation was based on an improvisational jazz sensibility that, as Eric stated, aimed to "get so far away from the original line that you're playing something that's never been heard before."[2] The intention to make a double album that could reflect this dual nature of the band was almost automatic. One part of it would consist of tracks the band wanted to record live, expressly at the Fillmore.

The Bay Area would have been the background where, within less than a year from Cream's first arrival there, live experience and live recording would blend and coexist in the band's history.

This passage would have never happened, hadn't Robert Stigwood strongly wanted to get Cream signed by Ahmet Ertegun's Atlantic Records. Cream had recorded their second album, *Disraeli Gears*, at Atlantic Studios in spring 1967, but they weren't under any contract with Atlantic Records. As Cream's road manager Bob Adcock remembers, Atlantic's president Ertegun clearly didn't like Cream: he thought them too loud, and considered their music "psychedelic hogwash." He was only interested in Eric, and unfairly thought of Jack and Ginger as mere sidemen. Adcock also points out that, despite the general criticism often aimed towards Stigwood, it was thanks to him that Cream were eventually signed by Atlantic: Stigwood had an ace up his sleeve called the Bee Gees, whom he had been managing since 1967, and knew they were the band that Atlantic had laid its eyes on. But Stigwood would have never given them away just like that: on the contrary, he refused to sign the Bee Gees to Atlantic unless Ertegun also offered Cream a recording deal. In the end, it was thanks to Stigwood's inflexible and no-compromise attitude that the skeptical Ertegun was eventually won over, and Cream entered in the Atlantic roster. This made the realization of *Wheels of Fire* possible—the first double album to become gold and probably the best representation up to that point of a band captured live.

The live soundboard takes featured in *Wheels of Fire*, wouldn't be the only output generated from that experience; Cream were also filmed by Tony Palmer and featured in his documentary *All My Loving*.

Professionally filming live performances was still a novelty at the time. More than for technical reasons, it was rather for a little collective historical awareness, or, more likely, for the professional detachment among most of the media toward what was happening.

There was, indeed, an exception represented by independent filmmaking; a decade before the time frame in which Cream appeared, watershed cultural moments were captured on film in a totally new and revolutionary way by Direct Cinema exponents, all the way through the 1960s. From Bert Stern and Aram Avakian's *Jazz on a Summer's Day* and Murray Lerner's *Festival!*, respectively about the Newport Jazz Festival in 1958 and Folk Festival editions from 1963 to 1965, a new cinematic sensibility managed to represent the essence of pivotal cultural events, poetically meddling between performers and the audience. This tradition would reach its expressivity with D. A. Pennebaker's *Monterey Pop* and Albert Maysles, David Maysles, and Charlotte Zwerin's *Gimme Shelter*, on the Altamont free concert on December 6, 1969.

Such examples of filmmaking, unlike those produced by the "official" media outlets, rejected commentary, voice-overs, and all those features that contributed to a rhetorical and a too-analytical approach that only drifted from the essence of what wanted to be represented.

Audiences knew but had a totally different approach to that reality; they would live the event rather than break the experiential flow to take pictures, checking their cassettes or reels, or film on 8 mm. We will see further on in this book that there were indeed those who would go to concerts to immortalize them in some form, at least a few at every concert, but compared to the event in its complexity and to the number of people in the audience, it was a small thing. Given the conditions in which most such happenings took place, it is almost a miracle that, to this day, anything was recorded at all and survived. After all, witnesses remember that time almost as something that was over before anybody knew what happened, it was so unique and intense.

Neither were the most sensitive and eminent of the chroniclers of that era, such as photographer Jim Marshall, really aware of the historical impact that what they were immortalizing would have in the future; in 2006, at an interview at Wolfgang's Vault, photographer Michael Zagaris asked Jim Marshall, "When you were doing all this, did you have any sense that at some point in time these pictures would be so important?" Without batting an eyelash, Marshall replied, "No. I really didn't. I was doing it as a job, but guys like us were documenting history, a part of our country's history."[3]

From what we can gather from Jim Marshall's and many of his contemporaries' accounts, a great part of what is left today of any professional footage and film shot in the 1960s, which is in fact very scarce compared to the rich flow of events that was unfolding, was made because it was just "work." As regards the filming, this same perspective implied that what was captured was generally brief and sketchy. Furthermore, scarce archival conscience or small departments' available capacity led to many of the unused film rushes being thrown away. Longer footage than the one that was finally used for TV news or special broadcasts was never to be seen again, by anyone.

Just like it happened with photojournalism, this process was just ordinary business: assignments were filmed or photographed, editing was done (or, in photography, proofs were checked to see what could be printed), and finally, just like unused shots were discarded without ever looking back, film rushes were thrown away.

Luckily, among reporters and TV broadcasters there could be personalities who felt that what they had before them was making history, and would therefore give their footage an auteur, self-aware take. This is the case with English director and producer Tony Palmer.

At the time Cream appeared on the English music scene, Tony Palmer had been producing and directing many films and programmes for the BBC about arts: Isadora, about dancer Isadora Duncan, directed in 1966 by Ken Russell; The Art of Conducting, in 1966, with maestro Georg Solti; Benjamin Britten & his Festival, in 1967, and on the same year, Twice a Fortnight, featuring the most interesting acts in pop. Classical music and popular music - Benjamin Britten and Cream? Quite an unusual combination for the time, isn't it? Still, Palmer, an eclectic intellectual and insightful expert in music, proved to be above the frequent and sterile debate on music genres, which separated in a rather Manichean manner "good" from "bad" genres, or "elevated" music from "low" music, and theorized the equal dignity of pop to classical music. He even came to acknowledge pop as the new classical music. With this perspective, Palmer went against a pattern of thought introduced in 1966 by Theodor W. Adorno in his Negative Dialectics, according to which some music genres were more dignified than others; in particular, pop music was disparaged by the German philosopher as opposed to the more elevated jazz and classical music and was part of a scheme that Tony Palmer, quite innovatively and programmatically, proceeded to go against. He almost seemed to embrace, on the contrary, romantic philosopher Friedrich Schlegel's theory of the cyclic nature of genres: for the fact that literary genres are bound to reiterate themselves through history, similarly, classical music has reiterated itself in modern times in the form of pop music.

Tony Palmer's revolutionary vision would be represented in a BBC documentary he would direct and call All My Loving.

All My Loving was far from a simple music TV special broadcasted by the BBC: it is the first manifesto of pop music and comprises interviews, live performances, and declarations on the role of pop music in the society of the time, by the most-representative artists of the British underground music scene. In 1967 and 1968, some of these bands were touring America, leading the last wave of the British Invasion phenomenon that swept the States in 1964 with the Beatles. Tony Palmer followed some of these musicians through the Continent with his BBC troupe, on and off the stage, delivering us the only existing proof on film of certain performances. That included Cream, whom Tony met in San Francisco in February 1968.

San Francisco, February 29–March 3

When Cream met with Tony Palmer in San Francisco, they had just ventured into their second major US tour, playing Santa Monica on February 23, Santa Barbara on the twenty-fourth, and San Bernardino on the twenty-fifth.

Tony met with Cream on February 29, the first day of a long series of eight live appearances in San Francisco up to March 10.

This series of shows, all promoted by Bill Graham, divided into two tranches: the first went from February 29 to March 3, while the second went from March 7 to 10.

Unlike the last time Cream played in San Francisco, these new shows wouldn't be played only at the Fillmore: on their first night of the first run of concerts, February 29, Cream would play Winterland.

Winterland was a large venue built as the New Dreamland Auditorium in the 1920s, an ice-skating rink that hosted the Ice Follies but also opera, boxing, and tennis matches. Bill Graham started to promote concerts there after attendances began to grow in number at the Fillmore Auditorium, which put him in need of a wider hall. With its 5,400-seat capacity and location on Post and Steiner, literally only a block away from the Fillmore, Winterland proved the best solution to Bill's needs.

In their first run of shows in 1968, Cream played Winterland for three nights, February 29 to March 2, and returned to the Fillmore for the final night on March 3.

Tony Palmer realized that Winterland could give him and his BBC troupe more room to properly film the band than the smaller Fillmore; therefore, the footage of Cream for *All My Loving* would have been shot there. He wouldn't only film the band onstage at Winterland but would also do interviews with Eric, Jack, and Ginger. These interviews were initially done and filmed for *All My Loving*, but eventually they didn't make the final edit and ended up in the later Cream's *Farewell Concert* film at the Royal Albert Hall. These interviews would become probably the most representative for each member of the band, especially for Eric Clapton, whose demonstrations on his "Fool" Gibson SG would inspire generations to come to take up the guitar.

Controversy has been surrounding the whereabouts and dates of the Cream footage Tony Palmer filmed for *All My Loving*. On the basis of recent conversations and archival research, it has emerged that interviews of each band member, plus some of the live footage, were made at Winterland on March 2. Additional live footage was also shot at Winterland, but on March 9.

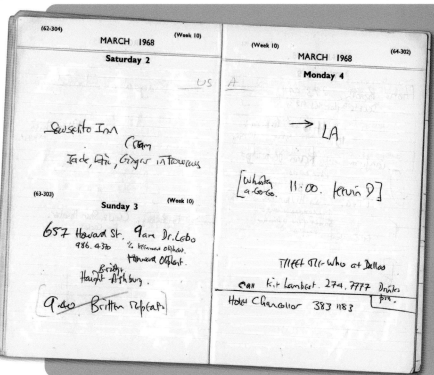

Pages from Tony Palmer's 1968 diary. As can be read, interviews with Cream (later featured in the Royal Albert Hall film) were done on Saturday 2, 1968, before the Winterland performance.

However, Tony got it straight: filming Cream onstage wasn't all that made his time with them in San Francisco special. In a recent interview, he told me more about it:

For me, what was really memorable about that occasion was spending time with them at the Sausalito Inn. It was a quite small little hotel, which is right across the Golden Gate Bridge. They were extremely relaxed, very jolly, and we chitchatted away for hours and then we did the interviews. I did long interviews with each of them, which I originally filmed for *All My Loving*, but eventually used them in the Cream *Farewell Concert*, and in every known version of the Cream *Farewell Concert*. I did these three interviews where Ginger demonstrates on the drums and complains all the time, "Bloody difficult this time of the day!"—very funny!

Eric is fantastic there, and he gives an example of how he forms various blues riffs, and also he says on one point, "I try to get some of my aggression out from the way I play," and he gives a demonstration.

Jack also is very interesting about his social background. He came from the slums of Glasgow; his father was a Communist trades union man.

So, in a way, that for me was more interesting than simply watching them on stage, although that was pretty amazing too, but those three interviews, that's absolutely the right time, and you can take screen grabs of each of those interviews and you got precisely that period of time when they were there. Sadly, each of the interviews was much longer, and of course the BBC junked all the material except what you see in the film.

When we did a film later with Jack called *Rope Ladder to the Moon*, partly about him going back to Glasgow, we tried to find some of that interview. I was asking him questions, when he said, "Didn't we talk about all that in San Francisco?," and I said, "Yes, but I don't have that material anymore." And of course, partly as a result of that, not of me filming him at Winterland but as a result of getting on extremely well with him in the Sausalito Inn, came the invitation to film the farewell concert, which of course was only a few months later.[1]

Tony soon realized that Cream was just one of the many extraordinary things happening at that time in the Bay Area; just like Eric Clapton remembered, there was "a whole kind of circle of events that would surround us each time we were in San Francisco."[2]

Back then, San Francisco represented the undiscussed epicenter of musical, cultural, and societal turmoil, working as fertile ground for innumerable forms of expression, new lifestyles, and values. The Haight-Ashbury neighborhood in particular was the backdrop where a new collective consciousness, influenced by LSD and drugs in general, had started to emerge. An important manifestation of its emergence from the underground to everyone's recognition took place on October 6, 1966, the day LSD was made illegal. To this news, the neighborhood responded with a free concert named "Love Pageant Rally" in the Panhandle area near Golden Gate Park, where the Grateful Dead and the Jefferson Airplane performed. This get-together would lead to the first Human Be-In, held on January 14, 1967, at the Polo Fields in the park, marking the complete self-recognition of the Haight-Ashbury neighborhood as a scene, an organic community. Such gatherings would become a collective ritual, especially in the Panhandle, where local bands would perform impromptu sets for hundreds of people. It will come as a strange surprise to those who read this, but Cream have also been reported as playing an unadvertised set in Golden Gate Park. Apparently, Cream were seen playing in the park one afternoon between the two Fillmore appearances of March 3 and March 7. As San Franciscan Jeff Godoy reported, "We were on Haight Street and someone came by and said Cream was going to play in the Park; they were set up like a local band on the grass."[3] Unfortunately, no audio or photographic proof has surfaced so far to validate this information.

Special as it may look and sound today, when Cream was in the city, it was "just another week" for San Francisco, but one to remember for the band and Tony Palmer in particular:

> If you lived in San Francisco, in Haight-Ashbury, it was more important being part of the experience than to figure out what was going on. One of the weirdest things that happened when we were making *All My Loving* happened on March 3, the day after I interviewed Cream and filmed them at Winterland: we were in Haight-Ashbury and there was a crowd. We weren't quite sure what the crowd was for, because there was always a crowd in Haight-Ashbury, when suddenly a truck arrived, like a furniture van that was open in the back,

and we could see this group setting up. So, we started filming. I had no idea what the hell it was, so I asked who they were, and they said they were the Grateful Dead![4]

In the afternoon of the day Cream would play the Fillmore, Tony and his troupe found themselves witnessing a historic moment for the city: the Dead had set up a flatbed truck on which they would perform an unannounced, free concert that would mark their salute to the Haight. The Dead had been inhabiting their historical "headquarters" on 710 Ashbury Street since October 1966, but by March 1968, all of them had already left the neighborhood after hostilities had started to manifest and had made the area a very different scene than it used to be. Harsh confrontations between the police and the citizens had started to ensue after Mayor Joe Alioto practically declared war on a neighborhood that until then had been the beating heart of the counterculture.[5]

Another occasion in which Tony Palmer found himself with his troupe in the right time and place.

Tony Palmer filming San Francisco for his *All My Loving* documentary. *Tony Palmer's film* All My Loving

The Grateful Dead bidding farewell to Haight-Ashbury with a free concert on Haight Street on March 3, 1968. *Tony Palmer's film* All My Loving

Oddly enough, from what can be read and heard about the first three performances at Winterland, the return of Cream to San Francisco didn't seem to meet the anticipation that had been building up since the last time they came there. Attendee Samuel James Parisi even recalls about seven or eight very large, hand-painted, hand-held "Clapton is God" signs inside Winterland on Saturday, March 2, rising as the band went on. Yet, Philip Elwood, who attended the first Winterland show on February 29, called it "disappointing" in the *San Francisco Examiner* on March 1.

Even Tony Palmer remembers as rather chaotic the first Winterland nights, especially March 2, which he filmed for *All My Loving*:

To be perfectly honest, they weren't that good! Partly because it was always a shambles at Winterland, the sound was never properly rehearsed, microphones were all over the place, there was a crowd that didn't seem to know who anybody was. Additionally, they were stoned on every known substance, if you see what I mean! If I say they didn't take their performances that seriously at that time, that's a bit of an exaggeration, but there's an element of that in it, you know; it was just the next stage on the tour. They didn't think, "This is Winterland, my God; this is the home of rock and roll; we've got to perform wonderfully!"

They didn't approach Winterland with anything like, "This is the holiest of holies"—it was just another concert. I don't in any sense want to diminish the extraordinary music that they made, or could make, or did make, but the notion that it was sort of part of some master plan that they turned up at Winterland because it was the holiest of the holies is nonsense—it is just not how it happened. It is not the experience that they possibly hoped for. And whatever substance the audience was on, they were definitely out of their brains; I don't think they had any idea who was playing.

It was always a shambles for rock-and-roll groups on tour those days. Do you remember the part of the microphone that kept dropping off while Jack was singing in *All My Loving*? That shows you how shambolic it all was! The Who would arrive in their bus and all their equipment, and all their costumes and all their things were in this Greyhound bus,

so you can imagine how small their sound equipment was. I mean, you'd have an amplifier the size of a suitcase, more or less! The Beatles were lucky because not only did they have this father figure called Brian Epstein, but they also had two absolutely devoted roadies who'd look after all their gear. So, they were organized; most tours were not. Most groups knew what they had to play, they knew what time they had to play, but that was about it. They would end up with faulty equipment and a sound system that often broke down. When I made *Bird on a Wire* with Leonard Cohen, the sound system just broke down on several nights! It was held together by chewing gum, and you just hoped it would all work! One shouldn't underestimate the comparative chaos with which these events took place, when bands were touring night after night after night, and the only way to get around in the States at least was in a Greyhound bus!

The only good thing about Cream's farewell concert is that it was well organized, because they knew that it was it, and they had to get it right one last time. Until the stadium aspect of touring got underway, which was the end of the 1960s, it was, as we would say in English, a "kick-bollocks-scramble." I'm sure if Bill Graham was still with us, he would be the first to admit it.[6]

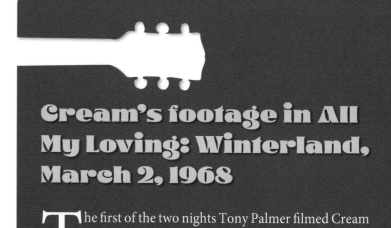

Cream's footage in All My Loving: Winterland, March 2, 1968

The first of the two nights Tony Palmer filmed Cream was at Winterland on Saturday, March 2, 1968. First in the morning, for each musician's interview, then onstage.

Winterland. Saturday, March 2, 1968. *Tony Palmer's film* All My Loving

Winterland. Saturday, March 2, 1968.
All photos by Paul Sommer

Winterland. Saturday, March 2, 1968. *All photos by Steve Fitch*

On the right in the last photo, there is a rare sight of Cream's manager Robert Stigwood, who came to San Francisco to meet the band at Winterland on March 2. Tony Palmer, also caught in the photo while filming the band, remembers:

Interestingly enough, one of the two nights we filmed them at Winterland, March 2, Robert Stigwood turned up, and I don't think they were expecting him. I personally got on very well with Robert, but it was clear there was a sort of tension between the three of them and him. I didn't know what the cause of this tension was at that time, I later found out that they all took the view that he was ripping them off. Of course, nobody said that at that time. It was very strange because, although he was their manager, he wasn't like Epstein with the Beatles or Peter Grant with Led Zeppelin, if you see what I mean. Led Zeppelin, and particularly Jimmy Page, knew perfectly well what Peter Grant had done for them, which was making them very rich, but you never felt that from the Cream towards Robert Stigwood. It was always, "How did we get involved with this guy?" And as Jack told me several times, "Does he think we're one of the Bee Gees?!" That's obviously because Stigwood was also the manager of the Bee Gees.

Jack, in a way, was the most intelligent of the three; the other two were very bright indeed in different ways, but Jack was almost intellectual. He came from the worst slum in Europe, from Glasgow, and he had been to the Scottish Academy of Music, so he knew his stuff, and he couldn't understand how this rock-and-roll group got muddled up with this Australian called Robert Stigwood! Imagine the slums of Glasgow to an Australian! It doesn't make any sense! There was backstage a very strange tension between the three of them and Robert Stigwood, which I was aware of, but I had no idea what the cause was at that point, but later on I realized it. After Cream had broken up, then I realized, when I went back to Glasgow with Jack, and I went across the Sahara Desert with Ginger, and then I got all the gossip, all the background stuff.[7]

Unfortunately, no audio recording has surfaced so far from those first three Winterland nights that could let us make our own idea of what Cream's first three San Francisco shows of 1968 might have sounded like—apart from the brief excerpts from "I'm So Glad" featured in *All My Loving* (of which the audio track is from March 2, while the footage is both from that night and March 9).

However bad what was said and written about those Winterland nights was, the same can't be said of Cream's return at the Fillmore on March 3—an incendiary, long, and experimental set from which a new, previously unheard recording has been found just recently.

The Fillmore March 3 concert has been known from a widely circulating bootleg series of Cream recordings named *Cream ReMasters*; this collection, together with studio outtakes and early live recordings, featured a CD titled *Live at the Fillmore*, containing one recording from September 3, 1967, and one from March 3, 1968. The taper, which was allegedly the same for both recordings, captured five songs on the March 3 night: the opening (an extended "N.S.U."), "Politician," "Sunshine of Your Love," "I'm So Glad," and "Stepping Out."

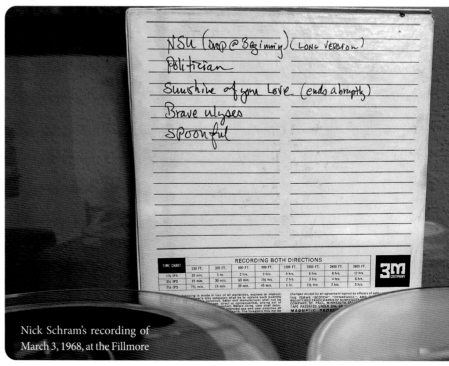

Nick Schram's recording of March 3, 1968, at the Fillmore

From a recent discovery I made of a different, totally new source from the same concert, we learn of a longer set list: two new songs add to the previously known titles—"Tales of Brave Ulysses" and "Spoonful."

Mixed together, these two sources make up the most definitive set list we have so far from the Fillmore concert on March 3, 1968—we're all hoping that new sources with more songs will come out one day!

FIRST SET
"N.S.U."
"Politician"
"Sunshine of Your Love"
"I'm So Glad"

SECOND SET
"Tales of Brave Ulysses"*
"Spoonful"*
"Stepping Out"

* previously unheard songs

The new, previously uncirculated tape from March 3, 1968, is only one of the many recordings made at Bill Graham's venues by a guy called Nick Schram, with whom I connected in 2018 while working on a previous book on the Who, subtitled *Concert Memories from the Classic Years, 1964–1976*.

Nick and his friends were weekly regulars at legendary San Francisco rock venues such as the Boarding House, California Hall, the Western Front, the Great American Music Hall, the Keystone Club, Avalon Ballroom, Playland, Berkeley Community Theater, the Fillmore, Fillmore West, and Winterland for hundreds of shows from 1965 to 1978. In 1968, Nick had a top-rated radio show on a progressive rock station in San Diego. He would go on to a very colorful and storied labor union career, which included a role in the infamous California Teamsters' Coors boycott with a couple of side trips into managing rock musicians.

From what we'll learn, Nick's story adds a whole new nuance to what has passed for the "official" underground dimension of the San Francisco scene, providing new, essential information that has been kept off the record until now. "We lived the second great cultural renaissance. We really were a random group of people who were in the right place at the right time in history," tells Nick.

Nick Schram's recordings of Cream at the Fillmore on March 3 and on March 10, 1968

"For instance, my wife's father worked for the printer who printed every Fillmore poster. Her brother-in-law worked for Bill Graham. We ended up with the biggest thing in FM radio history in San Diego. We saw everybody at Fillmore and Avalon Ballroom, never paying more than $10 a ticket for the Rolling Stones, Pink Floyd, the Who, Led Zeppelin. We were very professional about our approach. We realized in 1965 that this was the Second Renaissance, and it was our duty and desire to capture our favorites live / in person, but we also wanted our own 'live' records of the shows."

At this point it is important to understand the power of the record companies in the 1960s and early 1970s. Nick would record the shows he attended, then later play the tapes on his radio show. Because of how widespread the record companies' reach was into broadcasting, and the economic damage they could inflict on stations, Nick would back-announce a tune from a bootlegged Hendrix or Cream tape as having come from an "import" album. Thus, the record company attorneys and monitors would be thrown off the trail.

Anything but ordinary so far, but according to Nick, there is an important piece of background information that no one has delivered, regarding taping shows at Bill Graham's venues. It must be remembered that upon entering the *Bill Graham Presents* concerts, from 1965 to 1967, no one was ever searched. In 1968, they started searching and used the excuse of "safety," looking for weapons. In Nick's opinion, "That was a bullshit cover story to conceal the actual reason, which was to catch us bootleggers recording shows. There was never a weapon-related event or violence at a San Francisco concert until Altamont in December 1969. Consider this: Why would you undertake 'searches' for weapons of virtually 100% white concertgoers who shun violence and its 'tools'? No, it was us bootleggers they were searching for. Why was it so important? Because the record companies were freaking out, and Bill was doing it himself. So, if he appeared to be protecting the 'artists' and more importantly the labels' copyrights, no one could ever suspect HE was doing it."

So, how did Nick do it? Luckily, a US Navy mate of his was assigned to an audiovisual unit and had access to state-of-the-art small Uher reel-to-reel tape recorders and government-grade Nakamichi cassette recorders. Nick's wife would conceal the devices under bulky sweaters and coats and, later, maternity clothing. Once the "searching" started, as with traditional "smugglers" tactics, Nick would often create a slight diversion by appearing to try to bring in outside food, which would ultimately be confiscated while his wife walked by unnoticed. Once inside, they would head to the balcony and position themselves for optimum mic placement and capture the performances.

As Nick points out, "Another reason for the bullshit excuse is they didn't want to be explaining how these searches were not violating people's rights to be free from searches. So, they relied on the good old American fear tactics, guns. But at the same time, they never searched the Hells Angels." Nick tells of his recently departed friend "Irish," an associate of motorcycle gangs who was once being followed by the SFPD. They knew he was at the Fillmore. When they told Bill they were there to arrest Irish, Bill told them, "No, you are not arresting him in my joint; you can get him when he leaves." Irish left via the stage door.[8]

Nick also sets straight a "street" truth behind what has always been let on as the "official" reason—according to which, Bill, in mid-1968, decided to close the Fillmore Auditorium—for moving his productions to the Carousel Ballroom, renaming it Fillmore West, located in a "safer" neighborhood. According to Bill, "Martin Luther King's death forced me to start thinking seriously about moving out of the original Fillmore. . . . The streets in that area were so tough anyway. After the assassination and the riots that followed, white kids were afraid to come into the area."[9]

As Nick put it, "Winterland and the old Fillmore were virtually across the street from each other. We San Franciscans never were intimidated by, targeted by, or victims of the people in the Western Addition, as it is called." Nick has recently reached out to his former Fillmore mates, and fifty-plus years later the unanimous consensus is that no one ever experienced any unpleasantness attending Fillmore/Winterland concerts in the 1960s and 1970s. He also remembers his wife and him taking their five- and six-year-old children to Winterland to see Robin Trower in 1975.

As Nick continues, "The Carousel Ballroom / Fillmore West was just another venue. It was above Waters Buick and had been a ballroom dance venue. The riot/safety issue was a lot of 'folklore' bullshit based on racist views of the Black neighborhoods. Also,

Fillmore West was walking distance from David Rubinson / Columbia Records offices, and Bill's main *Bill Graham Presents* offices were around the corner on 11th Street, near Mission Street. The main areas that had the violence and street drug dealers were the Tenderloin District, Hunters Point, and Bayview. The Tenderloin, which happened to be the theater district, was also the location of another Bill Graham venue, the Orpheum Theater. That was *the* dangerous neighborhood. In the Fillmore District at that time, the Black people didn't care about us, and in fact they were both amused at all us long-haired whites and, like everyone else, were fascinated with hippie girls. In fact, we started noticing more and more Black people in the audience taking in the incredible kaleidoscope of musical delights for $2.50 a ticket."[10]

"It must be noted that, regardless of the way *Bill Graham Presents* staff conducted the business," points out Nick, "Bill was a true visionary and a true Renaissance Man. Bill guided our generation to musical and artistic excellence we never would have known. Bill may have started this revolution in San Francisco but soon exported his genius all over the world. A ruthless businessman, impresario, and a charismatic pioneer, Bill was also a caring and generous man."

Nick tells of a remarkable experience he, his wife, and two friends had in 1968 thanks to Bill's generosity.

Nick was an on-air disc jockey in San Diego, and he called Bill one day in October and asked him if he could reserve three tickets for the October 10 concert with Buddy Miles Express and Jimi Hendrix. Bill told Nick to ask for him when he got to the box office. Stepping off the short PSA flight, Nick was nervous about the casualness of the arrangement. Arriving at the box office and asking for Bill, a few minutes seemed to drag on, but suddenly Bill appeared at the box office door and said, "DJ, San Diego?," then opened the door and said, "Enjoy; no charge." Nick and his wife and friends then witnessed the first of the historic three nights.

The next day, at two in the afternoon, Nick and company picked out a spot on the sidewalk with dozens of other Hendrix fans in line to buy tickets.

Amazingly, where they were sitting on the sidewalk was right in front of the Wally Heider Remote truck, with Eddie Kramer and the band listening to the previous night's recording.

Suddenly Bill walks by to check on the band, when Nick jumps up and thanks Bill for the tickets for last night. Bill looks at Nick and says, "What are you doing out here with these *schmucks*, six hours early?" Nick tells him they wanted to buy tickets for that night. Bill, with a big smile, shook his head and said, "For Christ sakes, come with me," and takes the now party of four to the side entrance and says, "Go in there and have a good time and don't let the staff see you."

So, Nick and company scurried to the balcony, sat in the first row, and watched an almost two-hour sound check. Jimi led the guys through medleys of Beatles, Stones, and Beach Boys songs for about two hours, then left the auditorium. That meant Nick and company would then sit in the dark, empty auditorium for four more hours, absolutely stunned and speechless.

But that's not the conclusion. Nick and the other DJ went backstage that night to visit with their friend Buddy Miles. After some chitchat, Buddy said, "Come with me; let's go watch Jimi's set." Buddy escorts Nick to the stage and to a row of folding chairs behind the side-fill speakers and out of view of the audience. Also seated in this primitive VIP section were Boz Scaggs, Buddy Miles, Jimi Hendrix's father, Nick, and friend. As Jimi starts his set, Bill bounds up the stairs to the stage, carrying a cardboard box full of fried chicken. So, they all scarfed up Bill's chicken and watched another history-making Jimi Hendrix set. That was the night Jimi was joined by Traffic member Chris Wood and Herbie Rich on organ.

For this episode along with all the other hundreds of remarkable nights Bill created, Bill will always have a special place in Nick's heart.[11]

Nick's collection of live recordings includes hundreds of names and shows, the majority of which from the Fillmore and Winterland.

For that particular Cream concert on March 3, 1968, Nick remembers he managed to smuggle his reel-to-reel deck by hiding it under his wife's dress, pretending she was pregnant! It was a simple trick, but effective, without which we wouldn't have the most complete version of Cream's last date of their first string of shows in San Francisco of 1968.

The band would return onstage on March 7, with the purpose to record some of the best music ever played.

One and a half years later after the band's forming, and thousands of miles away from home, on March 7, 1968, at the Fillmore, Eric Clapton was unconsciously fulfilling what he declared was Cream's first purpose: becoming "happenings on stage." Eric's take on "happenings," as we suggested in the beginning, must have undoubtedly been more literal than what is offered here, but it introduces an interesting coincidence. Cream brought a jazz attitude onstage that made every set they played unique—especially those they played in San Francisco, where they had the chance to play freely for the first time in their career.

Cream were 80% improvisation, as Ginger Baker pointed out, in that none of them knew where their playing would go.[1] This fact represented, at the same time, the band's blessing and its curse.

When they returned to San Francisco and recorded live tracks for *Wheels of Fire*, Cream were still at the beginning of a tour that would last until June and that, by its end, would have taken its toll on the band.

Eric remembered that second US tour as a "punishing schedule,"[2] where Cream were working in such an intense way, night after night, that they finally reached a burnout they wouldn't recover from.

Despite this, while in San Francisco between March 7 and 10, the band got the chance to enjoy some time off from the hard touring schedule: as Cream's road manager Bob Adcock remembers, "The highlight of our stay was taking a chartered yatch trip around San Francisco Bay, which was laid on by Cream's manager Robert Stigwood. David Crosby turned up at the quayside as we were leaving and provided a whole day's supply of 'smokables' which made the trip very 'interesting' . . . " Bob also admits the band staying at the Sausalito Inn was a great relief, as it made them avoid the bustle of downtown San Francisco. "I was no fan of San Francisco in those days," concludes Bob; "it was interesting to see the effect that Cream's performances at the Fillmore and Winterland had on their audiences though." [from a conversation with the author on March 27, 2022].

The recordings of the four nights at the Fillmore and Winterland were produced by Felix Pappalardi, whom Cream had first met in New York in April 1967 at Atlantic Studios, for the recordings of their second album, *Disraeli Gears*.

As Pappalardi might have probably felt, Cream's bravura and unique improvising formula hid their frailty, like something so perfect and intensely functional that wouldn't have gone too far before consuming itself; "The light that burns twice as bright burns for half as long," we might think.

Aware of this, Pappalardi probably felt the necessity to record Cream doing what they did best before it was too late: playing live.

What Cream would have played on those four nights was beside the point: what was more important was to record Cream per se, regardless of what music and how they could have played. The conceptual and aesthetic implication of freezing the frantic flux of an ever-changing creature such as Cream was stronger and more urgent than the strictly musical implications.

The four nights were professionally recorded by sound engineer Bill Halverson, who gives us interesting and exclusive information regarding his background and his majestic work for Cream in San Francisco:

I started as bass trombone player in high school at Temple City high school Los Angeles. Then in High School Senior I played in an orchestra dance band, in a junior symphony, and also in a dance band that a college teacher put together. We were a group of players from different high schools, and it was really a great band. One night, a friend of our college teacher came down to record us, and his name was Wally Heider. I learned a lot from him, and thanks to him I got obsessed with sound engineering. I really had wonderful people mentoring me.

That summer we played at the Monterey Jazz Festival and Wally recorded it. I tried to go to college, but finally my plate really took off, and I ended up in the Tex Beneke Band. I kept crossing paths with Wally: he happened to be running a studio for Bill Putnam in Vegas, and had a car and a trailer in which he recorded remote, and I started helping him do remotes when I would be in between tours. In early '64, I had a bad car accident, and Wally came to see me in hospital. It became hard to be a trombone player, since I had busted my wrist, and towards the end of the year I got fired and came back in LA trying to figure out what to do. Meanwhile, Wally had left Putnam's United Western, but still had the remote recording gear, so he said, "Come work with me!" We got a lot of jazz stuff, Woody Herman and stuff like that. I was getting better, helped Wally do a couple of rock bands, although he didn't much like rock and roll. Then he opened a little studio in LA, a little overdub room, got rid of the trailer and finally got a little truck in which we set up remote and all the equipment. We started with 3 track, 4 track, and then finally 8 track.

One day we got a call from Atlantic to do a remote at Fillmore in San Francisco and record Chuck Berry with the Steve Miller Band. Wally said, "Bill, why don't you take the maintenance guy and go do it?" So, I went and did it. I'd set up in a room in the club, learned my mistakes and got through that weekend.

After that experience, we got call from Atlantic to do this band up at Fillmore called Cream. Wally said, "Well, you did well with Chuck Berry, why don't you go up and do also this one?" So, me and the maintenance guy go back up there. Atlantic told me Cream had got trouble recording these English Marshall amps. When I got up there, I knew not to set up in the club, but in the truck. The roadies were there setting up, playing through the amps. I had a little Shure microphone which no matter where I'd put it, it just distorted! So, I panicked, as I was having real trouble getting any cleanliness. Nobody was there from the label, not even Felix Pappalardi, there was just me and the roadies at first. Of course, we had an 8 track: I got two Ampex mixers, one for the two audience mikes, and one Ampex mixer for the drums. The console had 4 tracks and that was two for vocals, one for bass and one for guitar. That's how we set up the 8 tracks.

I was moving the mikes around the amps, which were on 11—they just cranked! Finally, I went into the truck to listen: it was loud, but I wasn't contributing to the distortion. So, going back in, I realized that those Marshall cabinets had four speakers, and I ended up in the center of these speakers, and not in front of any of them. I did the same to the guitar and the bass.

Then slowly Eric and Jack showed up, they did a little soundcheck, which I recorded and thought, "Oh, we're gonna do ok!" It was loud, but, again, it's their distortion, not mine!

Wally Heider had a match set of Neumann 67 tube mic's that we used for audience mikes, so it was a deep good audience sound. We also had a splitter box for three mikes, so I split the three vocal mikes. Ginger had a vocal mike, but never used it, so his and Eric's mike were on one track, and Jack's was on the other one.

All of a sudden, walking in while Cream was doing some more soundcheck, was Tom Dowd and Felix Pappalardi. I said to myself, "Oh, Tommy's here, he's probably going to engineer this and I'm going to help him. It's all going to be ok!" Tommy and Felix asked, "Have you recorded any of the soundcheck?" I said, "Yeah, I got a little recording." "Let's go out and listen to it," they suggested. All of a sudden, Tommy went to Felix and said, "Ahmet's got me a meeting with Aretha down in LA, you're gonna do fine with Bill, I'm outta here! You don't need me." So, Tommy leaves and goes off. It's only me and Felix!

The other problem we had was, that string of shows had been booked for four nights at Fillmore. Bill Graham overbooked it, but Winterland was available. So, we had to do Thursday at Fillmore, tear everything down, go Friday and Saturday at Winterland, tear it all down again and go back to Fillmore for Sunday. I really liked Fillmore. We also did Janis Joplin there, Jefferson Airplane, Hendrix . . . It was a really good venue. Winterland was a skating rink, and we had to make it work and hope the PA guys didn't feedback, but eventually we got away with it!

I got an old vinyl of *Wheels of Fire* and I just cranked up "Crossroads" and "Spoonful," and . . . it's really good! Listen just to the ambience of the audience mikes. We had a really good PA guy, so there wasn't any feedback, and I had given Atlantic a good 8 track to record. Also, Wally didn't allow any limiters in the truck. As he taught me earlier on, even before the rock and roll stuff, if you put a limiter on a vocal, you're gonna get nailed! So, there wasn't any limiter on anything except for tape compression. It was 15 ips analogue, which is why Jack's bass got to sound fat. Another thing, you can't do any radical moves with live recording, because when you're mixing you have to undo it at the exact same spot. So, you pretty much at the beginning of the recording have to just really get it all just about right and just watch it to make sure that nothing gets out of hand. I had wonderful training from Wally to learn how to do that.

One of my fond memories from those March 7–10 days is when we were out in the truck with Felix and his wife Gail: there's no chair, we're sitting on the floor, wrapped up in blankets, and the recording is crank loud, and every once in a while, I turn around and go to Felix, "How am I doing?" and he'd go, "Yeah yeah yeah yeah!"

That's what we did for four nights.

I started to learn about production too, because Felix was very good about not playing favorites, not so much on the Fillmore stuff, but on the *Goodbye* stuff. Then we did the "Badge" stuff in the studio with George Harrison, and then I did Eric's first solo album, and in the mid-seventies did a nice solo album with Jack over in England. I didn't meet the guys while in San Francisco though. When I was called to do the *Goodbye* stuff, the first show we did was at Oakland Coliseum; I'm setting up and Jack Bruce calls me over and says, "Aren't you the bloke that did us last time?" I said yes, and he, "Oh . . . good!!" [*from a conversation with the author, June 29, 2022.*]

Wheels of Fire / Reels on Fire

Jack Bruce asserted that Cream was in fact two bands—a studio band and a live band. This dual identity would have been embodied in Cream's definitive album, *Wheels of Fire*, comprising nine studio tracks and four live tracks recorded at the Fillmore and Winterland throughout the band's four-night commitment.

The operation was pioneering and groundbreaking, in that the live recordings of Cream were among the first and, most of all, most-successful attempts to capture live rock music the way it was done by engineer Bill Halverson.

As Jack Bruce remembered, "Those were primitive days for live recordings,"[3] and Cream's live session represents the first time a large number of tracks from a recording, made with such an advanced equipment at a rock concert, was released in its unedited, unaltered form, despite the rumors around Eric Clapton's monumental solo on "Crossroads" being edited. It turned out that, in fact, it was not. They played *that* good.

Before Cream, the Beatles' *Live at the Hollywood Bowl* recording (1965), given the technical capabilities of the time, could not help but reflect the contextual condition represented by the 112 decibels produced by crazed audiences against the poor 100-watt PA; the Stones' *Got Live If You Want It!* album was an attempt to solve a similar problem through heavy redubbing. Bob Dylan's 1966 UK tour was recorded by the also-pioneering Columbia Records engineer Richard Alderson but could not be heard until 1970, when the first portion of it from Manchester (mislabeled as the "Royal Albert Hall concert") began circulating as a bootleg.

Likewise, the recordings on eight tracks of the Who at the Fillmore East on April 5 and 6, 1968, weren't heard until the early 1970s as a bootleg and had to wait until 2018 for an official release.

With such a premise, two sets per night for four nights, professionally recorded (except for March 8 at Winterland, when Cream played only one set), Cream could have had material to release for the next fifty years . . . had tragedy not struck ten years after those glorious nights at the Fillmore and Winterland.

On the night of February 8, 1978, Atlantic Records' storage facility was burned down by a fire that destroyed more than five thousand tapes containing session reels, alternate takes, and unreleased materials recorded for Atlantic and its sublabels between 1949 and 1969. The "facility" was in fact the former home of Atlantic's chief financial officer Sheldon Vogel's Department Store.

How could such negligence ever take place?

During the 1970s, as remembered by Atlantic president Ahmet Ertegun, Vogel came to him complaining about tapes cramming the label's Manhattan office, and suggested moving the material to the empty building in Long Branch, New Jersey, which belonged to Vogel's family. Vogel was on vacation when the fire struck.[4]

Such an event may only be adduced to scarce archivistic conscience and awareness, still diffused in the seventies; as the *New York Times* observed, "The preservation laxities were dictated by what seemed at the time to be common sense. For decades, the music industry was exclusively a business of now, of today's hot release, of this week's charts—of hits, not history." Adding, also, that "most senior executives in the record business have no understanding of what masters are, why you need to store them, what the point of them is. Crucially, masters were not seen as capable of generating revenue. On the contrary: they were expensive to warehouse and therefore a drain on resources. To record-company accountants, a tape vault was inherently a cost center, not a profit center." Strange as it may seem, such mentality could also reside at visionary labels like Atlantic.

Archive producer and director of archival research for various Eric Clapton documentary projects, including *Eric Clapton: Life in 12 Bars* and *Eric Clapton: Nothing but the Blues* Larry Yelen called the accident "a criminal act against art."[5] Producer Joel Dorn stated inside John Coltrane's box set *The Heavyweight Champion: The Complete Atlantic Recordings* that, with minor exceptions, every unissued pre-1969 Atlantic tape was destroyed.

Sound engineer Bill Halverson reveals a daunting and painful truth regarding Cream's live master tapes:

All the multitracks from the Fillmore, Winterland, and the *Goodbye* live takes went lost in the fire. Bill Levenson called me twenty years ago and said, "Do you know anything about any rough mixes of the *Goodbye* stuff?" because a guy brought a tape of one of the shows (we did three nights, Oakland, LA Forum, San Diego Coliseum), which turned out to be one of the 6 cassettes that I had made for Felix back in the day. What happened was that the last show was San Diego, and at the end of the night Felix said, "Can you make me cassettes of these three shows, so I can sort of prepare and see what I want to use?" I said, "Sure, and by the way, if I make you a set, can I make me a set too?" and he said, "Yeah, go ahead." So I did. When I got the stuff from San Diego back to LA, I went through it overnight and mixed down the whole three nights, roughly. I just set it up and let it run.

Then, apparently, a guy got hold of one of those cassettes after Felix died, and tried to sell it to Bill Levenson. When Bill asked me whether it was legit, I said it was, but he didn't need to buy it from that guy, because I got the whole set. So, Bill flew out to Nashville, we went into this mastering place, and he transferred all six cassettes to digital. What he transferred is what came out a couple of years ago in the *Goodbye* box set. The Fillmore and Winterland stuff, unfortunately, is all gone. [*from a conversation with the author, June 29, 2022.*]

The "case" of Cream's San Francisco live recordings seemed dismissed until 2018, when something new was discovered about those nights at Bill Graham's venues.

While searching for materials for my book on the Who, I came across a series of tapes and reel-to-reels containing audience recordings from those nights with Cream.

In particular, I received from Nick Schram, the DJ who used to work at KPRI radio in San Diego, two reel-to-reels containing unreleased songs from the Fillmore on March 10, which Nick recorded with his friend George Chacona. Some of these songs widely circulated for years as a bootleg by the name of *Wheels of Ice*: they were probably captured by some listeners while they were being aired by Nick from his KPRI station. Thanks to Nick's and George's recordings, we have been able to listen to tracks that otherwise, due to the Atlantic fire, we wouldn't know were played, such as "We're Going Wrong."

There is also another previously unheard audience recording made by Mark d'Ercole at Winterland on March 9, which I discovered and which Larry Yelen acknowledged in 2019 as "the first new Cream audio material to surface in a decade."[6]

Thanks to these recordings, a new light can be shed on those nights in San Francisco.

The following specifications about each night are based on the content of the tapes found by me and on the notes in the Atlantic Records logs, which are courtesy of Bill Levenson and Larry Yelen.

Fillmore Auditorium, March 7

FIRST SET
"N.S.U."
(according to Atlantic Records' logs)

"Spoonful"
(according to Atlantic Records' logs)

"Sunshine of Your Love"
(*After Midnight* limited-edition CD)

"Crossroads"
(according to Atlantic Records' logs)

"Rollin' and Tumblin'"
(*Live Cream* Vol. 1)

"Sweet Wine"
(according to Atlantic Records' logs)

SECOND SET
"Tales of Brave Ulysses"
(according to Atlantic Records' logs)

"Toad" (*Wheels of Fire*)

"I'm So Glad"
(according to Atlantic Records' logs)

(**"Stepping Out"** on *Live Cream Vol. 2*
could be from this night or March 8)

Fillmore Auditorium. Thursday, March 7, 1968. First set. *All photos by Nick Schram*

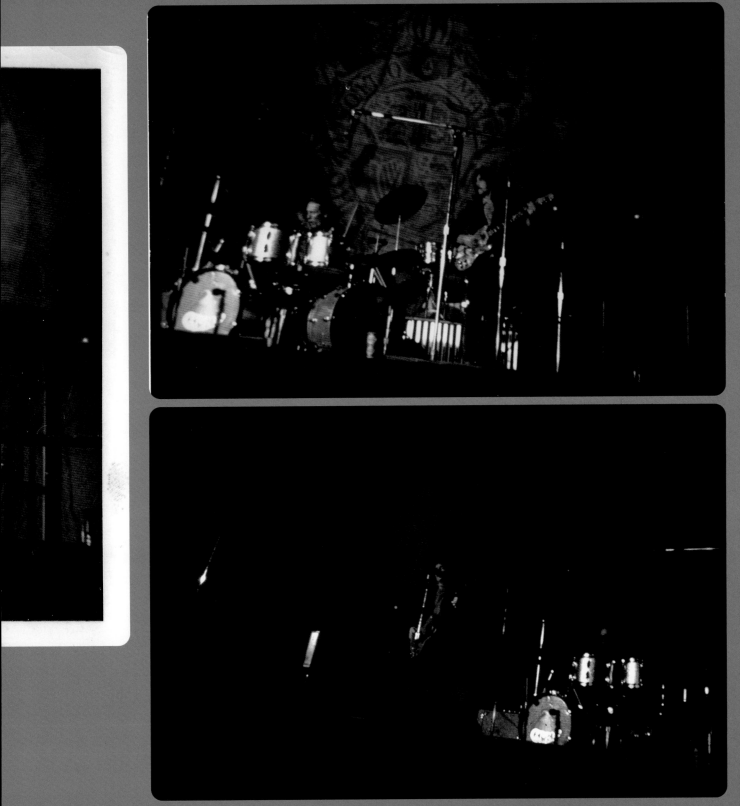

Fillmore Auditorium. Thursday, March 7, 1968. First set. *All photos by Nick Schram*

Fillmore Auditorium. Thursday, March 7, 1968. First set. *Photo by Nick Schram*

The flash seen in the photo above comes from this camera. Fillmore Auditorium, Thursday, March 7, 1968.

Fillmore Auditorium. Thursday, March 7, 1968. First set. *Photo by Nick Schram*

One of Nick's photos, taken on March 7, carries Eric's signature: he had Eric sign it at a party at the house of legendary Grateful Dead sound engineer and LSD manufacturer Stanley Owsley after Cream's show in Oakland on October 4, 1968. As Nick remembers, "I handed Eric a 10-inch-long Panama Red joint, which he proceeded to smoke entirely by himself!"[7]

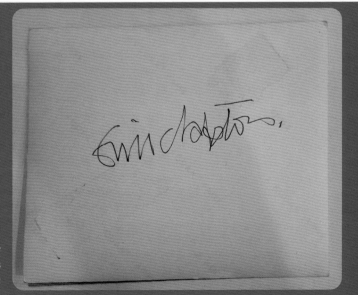

Eric Clapton's signature on the back of one of Nick Schram's photos. *Courtesy of Nick Schram*

Fillmore Auditorium. Thursday, March
7, 1968. *Photo by Frank Stapleton*

Fillmore Auditorium. Thursday, March 7, 1968. *All photos by Frank Stapleton*

Fillmore Auditorium. Thursday, March 7, 1968. *All photos by Frank Stapleton*

Fillmore Auditorium. Thursday, March 7, 1968. *All photos by Frank Stapleton*

Fillmore Auditorium. Thursday, March 7, 1968. *All photos by Frank Stapleton*

Fillmore Auditorium. Thursday, March 7, 1968. *All photos by Frank Stapleton*

Fillmore Auditorium. Thursday, March 7, 1968. *All photos by Frank Stapleton*

Fillmore Auditorium. Thursday, March 7, 1968. *All photos by Frank Stapleton*

Fillmore Auditorium. Thursday, March 7, 1968. *All photos by Frank Stapleton*

Fillmore Auditorium. Thursday, March 7, 1968. *All photos by Frank Stapleton*

Fillmore Auditorium. Thursday, March 7, 1968. *All photos by Frank Stapleton*

Fillmore Auditorium. Thursday, March 7, 1968. *All photos by Frank Stapleton*

Fillmore Auditorium. Thursday, March 7, 1968. *All photos by Frank Stapleton*

Fillmore Auditorium. Thursday, March 7, 1968. *All photos by Frank Stapleton*

Fillmore Auditorium. Thursday, March 7, 1968. *All photos by Frank Stapleton*

Fillmore Auditorium. Thursday, March 7, 1968. *All photos by Frank Stapleton*

Fillmore Auditorium. Thursday, March 7, 1968. *All photos by Frank Stapleton*

Fillmore Auditorium. Thursday, March 7, 1968. *All photos by Frank Stapleton*

Standing at the Crossroads, 1968

Fillmore Auditorium. Thursday, March 7, 1968. *All photos by Frank Stapleton*

Fillmore Auditorium. Thursday, March 7, 1968. *All photos by Frank Stapleton*

Fillmore Auditorium. Thursday, March 7, 1968. *All photos by Frank Stapleton*

Fillmore Auditorium. Thursday, March 7, 1968. *All photos by Frank Stapleton*

Winterland, March 8

Cream played only one set because Ginger was ill.

FIRST AND ONLY SET
"Cat's Squirrel"
(according to Atlantic Records' logs)

"Sunshine of Your Love"
(according to Atlantic Records' logs)

"Spoonful"
(according to Atlantic Records' logs)

"Traintime" (*Wheels of Fire*)

"Toad"
(partial—*Those Were the Days* box set)

"I'm So Glad"
(according to Atlantic Records' logs)

(**"Stepping Out"** on *Live Cream Vol. 2*
could be from this night or March 7)

Winterland. Friday, March 8, 1968. *All photos by Frank Zinn / courtesy of Rich Martin Frost*

Winterland, March 9

Together with March 10, this is the show that we have the most evidence of out of all four nights in San Francisco, thanks to an audience recording made by Mark d'Ercole.

From this, Cream can be heard hinting at "Cat's Squirrel" halfway through a long "Spoonful" jam.

Attendees state that the Saturday March 9 night was the biggest crowd ever seen at Winterland, to the point that side doors had to be open between acts to get some air.

Other than revealing new and exclusive information, Mark d'Ercole's Winterland March 9 recording in particular helps solve inaccuracies so far believed unthinkable; for instance, the true origin of the "Stepping Out" version featured in *Live Cream Volume 2*. Since the album's CD version appeared, "Stepping Out" was referred to as having been recorded on March 10, 1968.

If Nick Schram & George Chacona/*Wheels of Ice* bootleg's recording already ruled out that the "Stepping Out" version in *Live Cream Volume 2* could be from March 10, Mark d'Ercole's recording teaches us that the "Stepping Out" in question can't be from March 9 either. The two versions sound completely different from one another. Given the undeniable proof that Mark d'Ercole's and Schram/Chacona's recordings were made respectively on March 9 at Winterland and on March 10 at the Fillmore, then the "Stepping Out" version in *Live Cream Volume 2* must be either from March 7 at the Fillmore, or from March 8 at Winterland.

The March 9 concert at Winterland, recorded by Mark d'Ercole.

FIRST SET

"Tales of Brave Ulysses"
(Mark d'Ercole's audience tape)

"N.S.U."
(*Those Were the Days* box set; Mark d'Ercole's audience tape)

"Crossroads"
(According to Atlantic Records' logs)

"Sweet Wine"
(Mark d'Ercole's audience tape)

SECOND SET

"Spoonful"
(Mark d'Ercole's audience tape)

"Sunshine of Your Love"
(*Live Cream Vol. 2*; Mark d'Ercole's audience tape)

"Sitting on Top of the World"
(Mark d'Ercole's audience tape)

"Stepping Out"
(Mark d'Ercole's audience tape)

"Sleepy Time Time"
(*Live Cream Vol. 1*; Mark d'Ercole's audience tape)

"Toad"
(Tony Palmer's *All My Loving* documentary)

"I'm So Glad"
(silent-film parts dubbed with audio from March 2 featured in Tony Palmer's *All My Loving* documentary).

Eric at photographer Jim Marshall's apartment in the Richmond District, San Francisco, the afternoon of the March 9 concert at Winterland. © *Jim Marshall Photography LLC*

Winterland. Saturday, March 9, 1968. © *Jim Marshall Photography LLC*

Winterland. Saturday, March 9, 1968. © *Jim Marshall Photography LLC*

Cream's footage, All My Loving: Winterland, March 9, 1968.

The second and last of the two nights Tony Palmer filmed Cream was at Winterland on Saturday, March 9, 1968.

Winterland. Saturday, March 9, 1968. *Tony Palmer's film* All My Loving

Winterland. Saturday, March 9, 1968. *Tony Palmer's film* All My Loving

Winterland. Saturday, March 9, 1968. *Tony Palmer's film* All My Loving

It was 1968; I was a year out of St. Ignatius High School in San Francisco. I worked as a young (nineteen-year-old) salesman at Don Wehr's Music City, the hippest music store of that or any time. Don had Santana, Big Brother, the Dead, Quicksilver, and anybody who was anybody as his store accounts. Don was decked out with huge mustache and the latest duds at all times.

One of the perks to being the young "guitar know it all" was that on weekends the local ballrooms, the Fillmore, the Avalon, and California Hall, all would rent various pieces of gear from Music City. We delivered tons of stuff in the Music City van, Fender Twins, Hammond B3's (groan) big acoustic bass amps, the works. The after-hours driver would get an extra $20 and get to stay for the show.

At the Fillmore, Bill Graham's ballroom, you could deliver the stuff . . . and if they needed another stagehand you could not only stay for the show but be onstage and backstage . . . as long as you behaved yourself and actually helped out. I took advantage of this generous situation whenever possible.

March 7th, 1968, approached and was duly noted on my calendar. My heroes, Cream, were playing at the Fillmore and Winterland through March 10th. I was absolutely beside myself; I'd seen their first US tour and was impressed to death (along with every other guitar player in the world) and was getting my finances together to see how many nights I could go.

At nineteen years old I had a lot going on; I was enrolled in San Francisco City College (which I attended sparsely as possible), had a steady girlfriend, had my part-time job at Music City, took guitar lessons and practiced furiously and needed to keep the smoke and mirror show going to make the parents think I was contemplating SOME form of gainful employment . . . but energy? . . . man, I had energy.

About two weeks before their four-day stand, I was at my City College Tennis class . . . (hey, we all make mistakes, okay?) and the court was a bit on the wet side . . . and going for a wide ball (make your own jokes) I slipped on one of the rain-slicked painted lines . . . and kaboom! . . . came down on my left wrist . . . and broke one of the little bones in there . . . like, ouch, man.

Winterland. Saturday, March 9, 1968. *All photos by Billy Stapleton*

So, I get plastered up (fitted for a cast) at the doc's from my wrist, past my elbow! Great. As the weeks wear on, little slows me down and I'm doing all my activities (sans guitar playing).

Well, as luck would have it, Don Wehr comes to me and asks if I can manage the weekend delivery to Winterland with the cast on my arm and all. I believe it was three stacks of Marshalls for one of the opening acts, "Jeremy and the Satyrs" (horrible); they were from New York and insisted on renting Marshalls (unheard of in those days). Don had originally turned them down, but then someone waved big wads of money at him . . . PLUS . . . as a provision to the rental, Don insisted that they pay ME $20 extra a night (plus the delivery fee, we're talking $40 a night here, kids) to babysit the stuff and make sure it came back in perfect shape. Jeremy was the opener and I can't remember a single thing about him, but his name is on the famous three-headed yellow poster of the concert (way to go, Jeremy!). Also on the bill, the James Cotton Blues Band and the original Blood Sweat & Tears, quite a show for 4 or 5 dollars.

So that Thursday we loaded up the Music City Van and I and my broken wrist was off to the Old Fillmore . . . and paradise. I knew all the stagehands, so getting some help with the gear

was no problem. I told family and friends I would be gone as much as possible and not to worry.

Wait a minute . . . you said "the Old Fillmore" . . . then you said "Winterland"?? Stapes, you old duffer . . . which is it? Has one of the big carriage bolts that holds your brain in place fallen out? No kids, wacky as it seems this day and age . . . Cream opened their shows in San Francisco . . . Thursday night at the Fillmore . . . and then moved across Geary Boulevard to the big venue "Winterland" for Friday & Saturday . . . annnnd back to the Fillmore for Sunday night. Why for? Rent at Winterland was most likely the issue. . . . Bill Graham watched every penny, very shrewd guy. The posters and biographies all say different stuff as to the venues and dates, but the most-reliable sources bear out my memory of Thursday night at the Fillmore, Friday and Saturday at Winterland and for sure . . . (you'll see why Sunday is indelibly etched) Sunday back at the Fillmore.

I found a friendly Fillmore stagehand that afternoon who helps me get the Marshalls upstairs (two flights). Marshall cabinets have two big handles, one at either end, so you really only use one arm if someone else has the other handle. I waited that afternoon, while Cream's two roadies, Micky and Peter, loaded

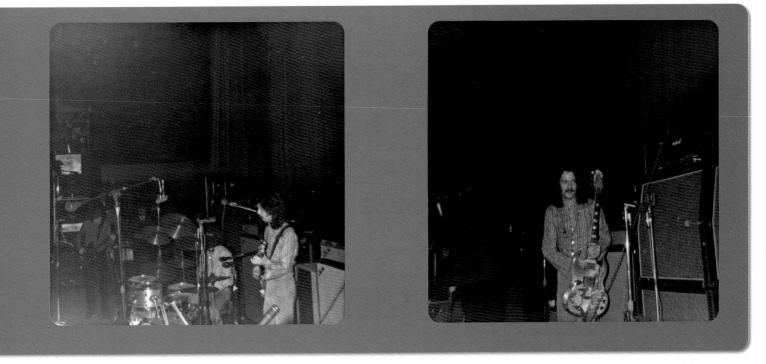

Cream's gear first up on the stage and watched in awe as they nailed Ginger Baker's drum set to the floor!!! (*fahbulous*) . . . the other acts' gear (backlines) went in front in layers that were removed as each act played . . . headliners in back.

I struck up a conversation with the two British, scrappy roadies and we soon became friends, joking and getting things set up. With everything ready, I drove the Music City Van back to the store, got my car, a '65 Ford Galaxy 500, and drove out to the Sunset district . . . home to my folks' house (at nineteen I still lived at home), had dinner . . . jabbered away incessantly about Clapton, etc. and split back to the Fillmore around 7:00 p.m., so I wouldn't miss a thing (told'jah I had energy!).

My first interaction with any of the actual band members was with Ginger Baker. A fearsome guy at times, he could just bore holes in you with those eyes. The opening acts had played, and he was onstage with the road crew getting his drum set comfy before they went on and turned to me.

"I want free Cokes . . . ," he uttered in spectacular Cockney.

"I'm not sure what your arrangement, regarding beverages, is with the people here . . . ," I began as apologetically as possible.

"No . . . I want free Cokes . . . ," he stated again with absolute command.

"Mr. Baker . . . if I have to BUY them MYSELF . . . you'll have Cokes!" I blurted.

Exasperated, Baker turned to face me and gruffly said, "NO! . . . I want free Cokes! One! . . . two! . . . 'free!"

The large lightbulb usually reserved for massive realizations went on with a visible spark in my young head. Baker didn't care whether I or anyone was paying for Cokes . . . he merely wanted three of them! (The Cockney "free" for "three" completely threw me).

Without further ado I scurried off for Cokes. That night, I sat on Clapton's side of the stage! . . . 10 feet from him . . . Marshalls singing their powerful arias . . . Cream at the height of their improvisational powers . . . the meat of their career . . . I was in HEAVEN! I tell yah. HEAVEN!

Well . . . just as everything was going GREAT about five songs into their set . . . Jack Bruce blows his two Marshall heads out! Blooey! . . . Cream is looking around for their two loyal roadies (Micky and Peter), who are not to be found! (. . . off getting loaded and chasing the San Francisco girls, it turns out).

So, who springs into action? That's riiiight . . . me.

I quickly move to Jack's side of the stage and pull the main fuse in his Marshall 100-watt Bass Plexi, and to my horror find a fuse-like length of heavy solid copper in the fuse socket. Apparently blowing fuses was something Cream frowned upon, so they just basically "hard wired" the safety fuse (everything they had was "plexi" as well (priceless, these days) . . . what the heck?)

Winterland. Saturday, March 9, 1968. *Photo by Billy Stapleton*

(Sorry, two-second tech lecture here). A regular amplifier fuse, 3 amp 4 amp, will blow to protect the amplifier's circuitry from damage in case of overheating, shorting, tube failure, or other circuitry malfunction. A length of solid copper in a fuse holder was something I'd seen many times before (no fuse? the show must go on!); that, and an old blown fuse wrapped in tin foil . . . and . . . if the amp wasn't workin' with one of these "hard fuses" in place . . . it only meant one thing . . . your amp was fried, brother.

So broken wrist & all, I replace Jack's two heads with two of the three we were renting Jeremy & the Satyrs (in front of a packed house at the Fillmore, stepping over cables and lights) and aawwwaaaay they went . . . back in business.

Winterland. Saturday, March 9, 1968. *Photo by Jeff Hawkins*

After the show (I am a hero), Jack Bruce comes up to me and sez, "Are you doing anything else this week?" in a lovely Scotch accent.

"Hoping to see you fellas a few more times," I replied. "Any night you'd like to come, you'll be our guest . . . thanks." Well of course I took full advantage of that invitation, and I was "in." And when Cream moved to Winterland Friday night, I was in the fold, mate.

Not only was I now a "behind-the-scenes guy" at the rock event of the year, but local recording wizz Wally Heider had his huge mobile-truck recording studio outside and patched directly to the stage. Recordings from these four nights would become the "live" record in the two-album set *Wheels of Fire*. Could it get any better??

Friday and Saturday night were just the best; the band played superbly, light show goin', the whole deal, man. Before their set on Saturday night, I was moving stuff around onstage, when promoter Bill Graham, who was looking at his watch (who knew me for years as the "Music City kid"), . . . told ME . . . to "go tell CREAM" . . . that they were "on"! Now there's a cool errand for yah. So, I run like a rabbit though the crowd and into the backstage area. The first two dressing rooms are filled with imbibing, bedecked revelers . . . some famous . . . some not so. In the third dressing room . . . lights down low . . . no one but Eric, Jack, and Ginger . . . huddled around a small black-and-white TV set, Cream . . . glued to the set . . . as they watch Paul Newman and Jackie Gleason in *The Hustler* . . . they'd never seen it!

I approach warily . . . as quietly as I could . . . I tell them they're "on" . . . Eric raises a hand (still glued to the TV) to let me know he's heard, and I tiptoe out and head back out to the main stage.

Well . . . about five minutes later . . . Bill Graham steams up to me and sez, "Where the fuck are those guys?" As only Bill could say it. "They're watching *The Hustler*" . . . I state as evenly and honestly as possible.

There was no actual response . . . Graham's eyes bugged out and I knew somebody was gonna get yelled at . . . I was only happy it wasn't gonna be me. (Graham's temper was legendary, as we'll see). Bill bounded offstage to the dressing rooms like a track star . . . no more than thirty seconds later, Cream is sprinting towards the stage through the crowd . . . Graham hot on their heels still lecturing them sternly . . . but his words are soon lost in the cheering of the crowd as they spot the band . . . beautiful . . . they take the stage . . . Graham regains his composure . . . introduces them . . . and "Tales of Brave Ulysses" comes wah-wahing out through a dancing light show that runs across the stage and crowd, just like "tiny purple fishes" . . . I can't really forget it, kids.

They play their hearts out, . . . applause for solos . . . applause for ensemble improvisation . . . Eric plays "Crossroads" . . . they play "I Feel Free" . . . they do "Spoonful" . . . Ginger plays "Toad" . . . they do encores . . . they are GODS!!

Sunday morning . . . Eric wakes up with a beautiful woman (most likely afternoon) after huge parties that rage all over San Francisco's hippest of the hip until dawn. Cream has conquered San Francisco.

The equipment needs to be moved from Winterland to the Fillmore for Sunday NIGHT. I show up around four and find Peter arguing with a caretaker at Winterland who refuses to open a roll-up cargo door because of some stupid regulation, not union, not authorized, I can't really remember.

The BIG problem is all equipment trucks and other roadies are in Sausalito, where the bands are staying. There is some big problem with the Golden Gate Bridge, and traffic is snarled throughout the rest of the afternoon. There IS, however, a giant dolly (10' by 6' at least) with huge wheels, that we could move the equipment on . . . but it won't fit through the side door, a regular-size door, even sideways (it also musta weighed close to 600 pounds!). We need to open the freight door and get the dolly out . . . but we are refused.

Around six o'clock Eric Clapton shows up with a beautiful girl in tow, to fetch his guitar, which was left backstage, in their dressing room, on a sofa. (I had waited around for hours for the equipment issue to get resolved . . . I explored every nook and cranny of Winterland in that time . . . and yes, I was in their dressing room . . . and YES I played the painted SG, "the Fool" . . . as well as my cast would let me, it was just layin' there being magnificent . . . and I tell you I can still remember the feel of that guitar like it was yesterday . . . it played like a rocket, fellas . . . who ever set that thing up knew his stuff!)

"Mr. C" asks what's going on; Peter and I fill him in. Eric proceeds to tell us he and his girlfriend will go distract the caretaker and tells us to "break the lock" that goes through the chain of the roll-up door.

Winterland. Saturday, March 9, 1968. *Photo by Jeff Hawkins*

"Break it with what?" Peter asks . . .

Eric reaches into a wooden box that contained various shipping implements (crowbar, etc.) that was by the freight door, and sez, "This ought to do it . . ." And hands Peter (his trusted roadie) a nice-sized hammer!

Eric and the absolutely stunning woman he's with go off to distract the caretaker . . . and Peter . . . well, Peter takes a mighty swing at that lock . . . and it breaks apart like a teapot! (We had hoped the lock would just "open" as opposed to shattering; this left the "cover up" portion of the plan obviously in question.)

We had all the equipment piled by the door in case the trucks showed up . . . so we piled the stuff on the gigantic dolly, rolled the door up . . . pushed the dolly outside . . . rolled the door down

. . . and Peter and I gingerly pieced the lock back together and threaded it through the chain . . . we stepped out into the afternoon sunlight through the side door . . . just . . . in . . . time . . . to . . . see . . . a . . . young . . . kid . . . STEAL GINGER BAKER'S 1948 LEEDY LUDWIG SNARE DRUM! . . . AND TAKE OFF DOWN THE STREET! AAHHHHH!

When I was a young man, before my knee got mushed I could run like a freakin' deer, people. And I lit out after this kid for all I was worth . . . all systems go . . . I caught up quick and got right up behind him and grabbed his jacket collar . . . which is when he threw the snare drum INTO THE STREET! (Geary Boulevard to be exact). Peter, who caught up with us, had saved it from being run over! . . . I was dangling the kid off the ground, who was "I'm sorry, I'm sorry, I'm sorry . . ." There was a big hole in the snare drum head (perfect, can't wait to tell Ginger) . . . and Peter just sez . . . "Let him go . . ." I gave him an extra shake and turned him loose . . . he was gone like a jackrabbit.

Peter and I push the giant dolly across Geary Boulevard and up to the doors of the Old Fillmore. We begin loading all the gear up the front steps. . . . We are pretty beat by this time . . . but . . . the show must go on.

We're halfway through the load-in when Bill Graham himself comes out of his office, walks up to us, and wants to know what's going on. We tell him there's no trucks and all the other road crews are stuck in Sausalito, . . . it's just us . . . moving it all. Graham then asks . . . "Is there anything I can do to help?"

Let me take a second to say that Peter, Cream's roadie, goes about 5'6", maybe 150 pounds of absolutely solid muscle. He grew up working on the docks in Liverpool; has nice clothes, shoulder-length hair, and a good mustache; and is a very nice bloke . . . until . . .

Peter, sweating his way through his satin shirt, sez, "Well, could you give us a hand then?"

Graham, whose tough-guy-hair-trigger temper is famous, FLIPS! "Really? It's not enough I pay you people, promote the shows, fly you

Winterland. Saturday, March 9, 1968. *Photo by Jeff Hawkins*

over from England, collect the money, and pay the fucking acts . . . NOW you'd Like ME to Help Load the Equipment IN???" He's screaming at Peter now.

Peter, who doesn't like being talked to like this . . . and grabs Graham by his shirt front and lifts him to his toes, saying . . . "Look, PRICK! . . . you ASKED all friendly like, if you could help . . . now PISS OFF before I knock your soddin' bloody teeth out!"

Having seen Graham berate artists and support people alike, with great gusto, I might add, . . . I relished the sight of him, terrified of this little British dynamo. Waving his open hands like white flags in front of his face, he backed down immediately, repeating, "It's cool . . . it's cool, man!"

Peter released him and he scurried into his office and slammed the door (presumably locking it behind him). We loaded the rest of the gear in and finished around 7:00 p.m., when a bunch of support people showed up and helped out. We were beat. I had brought my dad's Kodak Instamatic camera the night before and had taken a bunch of pictures. I was spending my last night with my new friends, and it turned into quite a doozy. Cream had sold out every night, and Graham was mostly pleased.

The lock? Well, when Micky, Cream's other roadie, finally showed up with the trucks from Sausalito . . . along with the other acts and their crews . . . they went up to the freight door and tried the chain pull . . . just as the maintenance guy walked up . . . and the security guy showed up . . . and the lock disintegrated . . . as Micky barely touched it!

Micky was read the riot act, chapter and verse . . . he was absolutely aghast that he was taking the wrap for our vandalism . . . but he never blamed anyone else . . . he just denied any wrongdoing and took it.

A lock was bought, the lock was replaced, order was restored. Micky knew who must have broken the lock, but he said nothing

. . . until he caught up with US . . . but . . . when he saw all we'd been through . . . let it go . . . mostly since he hadn't been arrested!

Robert Stigwood, Cream's manager, was given all the information regarding the roadies' adventures . . . including Peter threatening to knock Bill Graham's teeth out. And was giving Micky and Peter a stern talking-to backstage at the Fillmore as Eric and his girlfriend came by . . . Eric at first gave Micky & Peter a look that said, "I could save you . . ." and kept going . . . to his credit he came back and said to Stigwood, "I told 'em to break the lock, okay?" and breezed off.

Stigwood still had a few choice words for Peter, for threatening Graham and all, but it was mostly for looks, as Graham had snubbed Stigwood when he had asked Graham for seats onstage, so Stigwood stood onstage throughout the concerts. I tell yah, folks, what all goes on.

The cast on my arm? I had everybody autograph it, Eric, Jack, Ginger, Mike Bloomfield . . . and yes . . . I still have it! I got a great shot of Eric that night with my dad's camera and Eric gave me one of the giant tortoiseshell picks he used at that time . . . plus a nice big autograph, which are framed on my desk, as I write this.

Jack's broken bass heads were tossed in the back of the equipment truck prior to Saturday's show, where two more were pulled from a STACK of Marshall heads . . . there musta been ten of 'em, extra cabinets too.

Ginger was pretty good natured about the broken snare drum head (we never told him the drum was stolen; he'd have killed us!); his other head had been nice and broken in; he wasn't exactly pleased . . . but, I had the guts to ask him to autograph the broken one! Which he did . . . (imagine) . . . and yes, that's on the wall in my den. Quite a weekend for a nineteen-year-old; I don't know if I ever got over it, really.

Winterland. Saturday, March 9, 1968. *Photo by Jeff Hawkins*

Winterland. Saturday, March 9, 1968. *Photo by Jeff Hawkins*

Winterland. Saturday, March 9, 1968. *Photo by Jeff Hawkins*

Fillmore Auditorium, March 10

Cream's last show in San Francisco was originally scheduled to be held at Winterland and was so advertised on posters designed by Stanley Mouse; however, a last-minute change of venue was made by Bill Graham to the Fillmore and was consequently advertised in the *Berkeley Barb* on March 8.

FIRST SET

"Tales of Brave Ulysses"
(Nick Schram-George Chacona recording; *Live Cream Vol. 2*; Bill Graham's recording on Wolfgang's Vault)

"Spoonful"
(*Wheels of Fire*; Bill Graham's recording on Wolfgang's Vault)

"Crossroads"
(Nick Schram-George Chacona recording; *Wheels of Fire*; Bill Graham's recording on Wolfgang's Vault)

"We're Going Wrong"
(Nick Schram-George Chacona recording; Bill Graham's recording on Wolfgang's Vault)

"Sweet Wine"
(Nick Schram-George Chacona recording; *Live Cream Vol. 1*; Bill Graham's recording on Wolfgang's Vault)

SECOND SET

"Sunshine of Your Love"
(Nick Schram–George Chacona recording)

"N.S.U."
(Nick Schram–George Chacona recording; *Live Cream Vol. 1*)

"Stepping Out"
(Nick Schram–George Chacona recording)

"Traintime"
(Nick Schram–George Chacona recording)

"Toad"
(Nick Schram–George Chacona recording)

"I'm So Glad"
(Nick Schram–George Chacona recording)

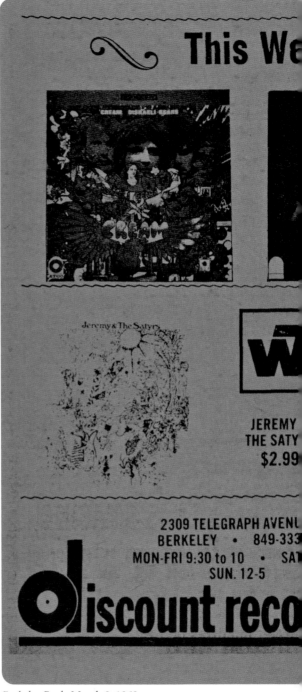

Berkeley Barb, March 8, 1968

Fillmore Auditorium. Sunday, March 10, 1968. Eric in the Fillmore dressing room with Steve Katz of Blood, Sweat & Tears, who opened for Cream on March 7–10. © *Jim Marshall Photography LLC*

Fillmore Auditorium. Sunday, March 10, 1968. © *Jim Marshall Photography LLC*

Fillmore Auditorium. Sunday, March 10, 1968. *All photos by Frank Stapleton*

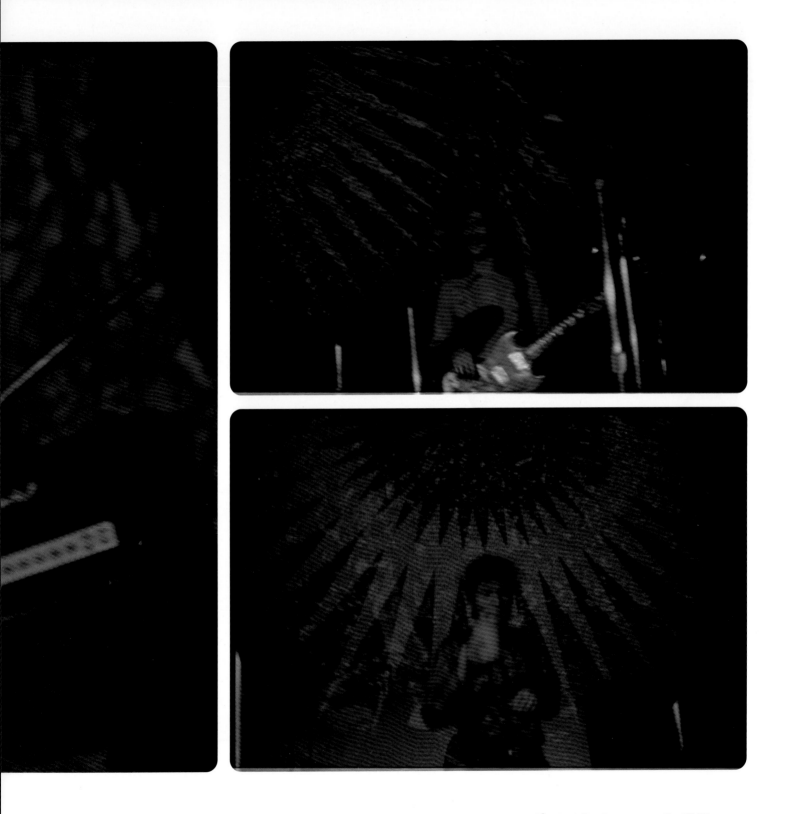

Standing at the Crossroads, 1968

Fillmore Auditorium. Sunday, March 10, 1968. *All photos by Frank Stapleton*

Fillmore Auditorium. Sunday, March 10, 1968. *All photos by Frank Stapleton*

Fillmore Auditorium. Sunday, March 10, 1968. *All photos by Frank Stapleton*

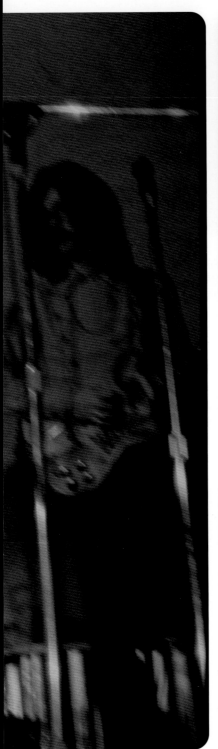

Fillmore Auditorium. Sunday, March 10, 1968. *All photos by Frank Stapleton*

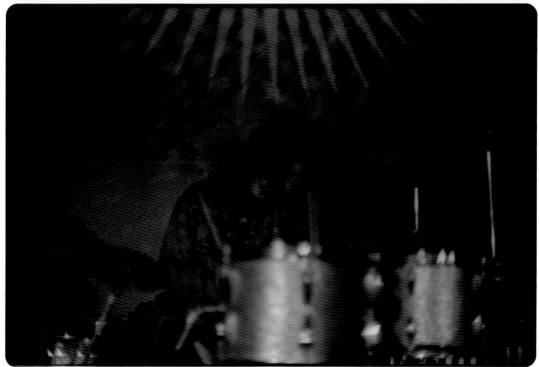

Fillmore Auditorium. Sunday, March 10, 1968. *All photos by Frank Stapleton*

Fillmore Auditorium. Sunday, March 10, 1968. *All photos by Frank Stapleton*

Fillmore Auditorium. Sunday, March 10, 1968. *All photos by Frank Stapleton*

Fillmore Auditorium. Sunday, March 10, 1968. *All photos by Frank Stapleton*

Fillmore Auditorium. Sunday, March 10, 1968. *All photos by Frank Stapleton*

Standing at the Crossroads, 1968

125

Fillmore Auditorium. Sunday, March 10, 1968. *All photos by Frank Stapleton*

Fillmore Auditorium. Sunday, March 10, 1968. *Photo by Frank Stapleton*

Fillmore, March 10, 1968
by Michael Lazarus Scott

This was my second time seeing the trio and there's some discrepancies about the dates and such, as I will try to explain. Having the band play San Francisco was a big coup for Bill Graham. He featured them for two weeks at the larger Winterland venue. I was gonna go, but just never made it across the bay. The last concert was a Sunday night and had been moved to the more intimate Fillmore. My friend Mike Mecartea and I decided it was our last chance and we had to go!

Cream's live record of the *Wheels of Fire* LP is credited with being recorded at the Fillmore show. I have always boasted that I was there when they recorded "Crossroads." I was told that even though the record itself says the Fillmore, it was actually captured at Winterland! Another said certain songs were recorded at each of the venues. I am not an authority, or person in the know, but the Fillmore was a much better sounding room and if you look at the poster, it appears they were gonna play Winterland for their final San Francisco concert, but apparently changed their mind? Bill Graham would have opted for Winterland as he stood to make more money. Anyway, I don't see how anyone is gonna prove me wrong and I'm going with the record! Mike Mecartea and I were at the Fillmore when Cream recorded "Crossroads"! So there!

Back to the story at hand; my best friend Michael Lindberg was a huge Cream fan and unfortunately never got to see them as Uncle Sam shipped him off to Vietnam. In his absence I met up with Mike Mecartea who became my concert partner. Always gotta have another Mike with me, even down to son Mike Scott who filled in later. All us nice guys named Mike tend to stick together! Anyway, I appropriated my dad's '64 Malibu SS and Mike and I headed off across the bridge. A quick mention was made that Blue Cheer was at the Avalon Ballroom on this fine night, but there was no contest there. I loved the original Blood, Sweat & Tears fronted by Al Kooper, having first seen Al in the Blues Project. BS&T was the first band of this hippie era to successfully bring a horn section on board, long before Chicago. Kooper has always been a unique innovator. Check out "I Love You More Than You'll Ever Know"! I don't remember this other group at all, but the old ballroom was buzzing in anticipation of Cream.

They most certainly did not disappoint. Jack Bruce most certainly in my top two bass players singing in his riveting Scottish brogue. Ginger in my top three drummers tapping out extraordinary patterns, with extreme precision and intensity. Clapton at his all-time best in every possible way, playing with the most authority and command over his instrument I have ever witnessed. He was the pure epitome of natural cool the intensity of each bent, stinging note registering on his concentrating face. He didn't need to jump around and put on a show. The music itself was the show. This was for myself, the coolest of Eric's many looks. The perm was gone and his mane was long and flowing along with his big gunslinger mustache and his great outfit. Then there's that psychedelic painted SG that brought it all together, the look and the sound. Mike and I, stalwarts that we are, were right up front with our mouths hanging open, at times staring at each other and shaking our heads in disbelief. It's difficult to convey how marvelous this performance was, but even though it was fifty-four years past, when I think about it, I still get chills. Saying it was great is a vast understatement.

That was the last time I saw Cream or Eric, but every time I hear "Crossroads," I always think about us three Mike's, the two of us that were there and the 1 that should have been . . .

My Cream Concert Memory
by Sandy Schram

Born and raised in San Francisco, and being in my teens during the Summer of Love, music was our love. I had the unbelievable opportunity to attend concerts every weekend performing at various venues by the greatest bands at the time.

When Cream performed in 1968, we were there. We (two married couples in our twenties) prepared ourselves for a long wait in line by getting to the Fillmore early so we could get first row seats in the center of the balcony for recording purposes. I was especially appreciative to have a "seat" being usually lost in a sea of people's backs at most concerts since I am less than five foot tall. This show would give me an unobstructed view of the band for the whole night! And since we would be standing in line for at least two hours prior to the concert, we brought homemade "snacks." The snacks kicked in just in time for the opening number.

I wore my usual hip-hugger, bellbottom embroidered denim jeans and a rabbit fur jacket and suede boots; quite the opposite to my daytime regular dress as a bank teller. Living by the "Establishment Rules" by day and loving the "Hippie" way at night was perfect for me.

The venue was packed and humming. The concert was loud and mesmerizing. Every song was exciting. There was barely a break between songs and then it was over. Good thing it was recorded by Nick so we could relive that night over and over again.

Don't You Notice How the Wheel Goes 'Round?

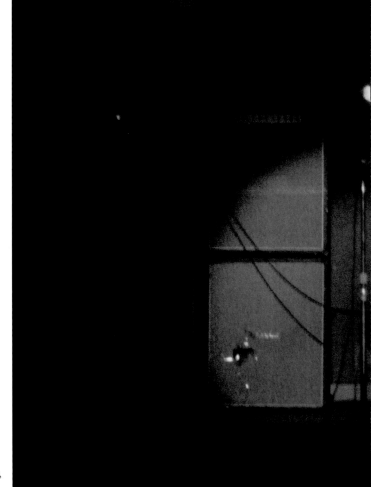

Memorial Auditorium, Sacramento,
California. Monday, March 11, 1968.
© *Jim Marshall Photography LLC*

Glorious as Cream's time in San Francisco may have been, something ominous was working behind the band's back. The three musicians' amazement and surprise before audiences' crazed reception soon started to wear away, because at every concert, in every city, the reaction was becoming the same. "We'd walk on stage to a standing ovation, before we'd even played a note," Jack Bruce remembered, "and that wasn't fantastic, because we'd been doing gigs we weren't happy with, and yet we'd get this enormous wave of adulation."[1]

Being exposed to an extremely tight tour schedule, which went from February to June 1968, with no time to renew themselves, Cream entered a sterile vicious cycle that started to suck them dry.

Halfway through the tour, Clapton told *Melody Maker*, "We've been doing two-and-a-half months of one-nighters and that is the hardest I have ever worked in my life";[2] years later, he would remember in his autobiography, "Whistle-stop touring America was the beginning of the end for Cream, because once we started constantly working in such an intense way, it became impossible to keep the music afloat and we began to drown. . . . When you are playing night after night of a punishing schedule, often not because you want to but because you are contractually obliged to, it is only too easy to forget the ideals which once brought you together."[3]

Betrayed ideals is what Cream had to face, especially because they were born "in a very idealistic way," like Jack Bruce remembered.[4] Like many idealistic things, they eventually wake up and succumb to a hard reality. Cream's tragedy lies in a pure, spontaneous, uncontaminated, innocent ideal being bent to music industry's logic.

Grande Ballroom, Detroit, Michigan.
June 7–9, 1968. *Photo by Allen Licari*

LICARI

Although much of Cream's tragic fate is often attributed to Robert Stigwood, portrayed as a greedy manager without scruples, he is remembered by road manager Bob Adcock as someone who in fact cared about the band, as demonstrates his tenacious efforts to get it signed by Atlantic Records. The demise of Cream perhaps is to simply attribute to an incompatibility between the band's vision and the music industry's ordinary modus operandi of the day. Cream's vision wasn't probably made for those times, or maybe for no time at all, and Cream as a group was probably a utopistic operation. Those were the days—like we said earlier on, for the better and worse.

Cream was based on a frail balance and needed to be looked after; it took both sympathetic and management skills to let the band grow and flourish more and always better. "Musically, we didn't really have a plan," remembered Eric. "In my mind, when I had fantasized about it, I had seen myself as Buddy Guy, heading a blues trio with a very good rhythm section. . . . The very idea that a guitar, bass and drum trio could make any headway in the era of the pop group was pretty outrageous."[5]

It was indeed outrageous and also anticonformist. Yet, Cream's anticonformism was put into pop's principles, and it was dilapidated.

"In a pop group, the first things you suffer from are jealousy and terrible insecurity. . . . You get really hung up and try to write a pop song or create a pop image. I went through that stage and it was a shame because I was not being true to myself." Instead, Eric "began to be quite ashamed of being in Cream. . . . It wasn't really developing from where we were. As we made our voyage across America, we were exposed to extremely strong and powerful influences, with jazz and rock[-]and[-]roll music that was growing up around us, and it seemed that we weren't learning from it."[6]

America slowly changed its face for Cream and went from almost being a protective, caring mother figure who gave them confidence, to being a ruthless and evil entity. Everyone in the band started to draw within himself and left the continent traumatized. From the two US tours there was but one year apart; yet, it felt like a long time since Cream first went out and, as Ginger remembers, "were supremely confident."[7]

"I've changed a lot through living in America," admitted Eric. "I've tended to withdraw from making contact with people. I'm harder to get to know than I was a few years ago. I don't trust people so readily."[8]

Pete Townshend, who was very fond of Clapton and would help him through one of the many periods of his life in the early 1970s, told the *Coshocton Tribune* newspaper on August 10, 1968, that "Eric has a very delicate ego. This US tour has almost turned him into a ghost." He also added, on Cream in general, they play so much in the US "they all have draft cards. And even though they make a big thing of improvisation, they've made so many one-night stands, their improvisation isn't improvised anymore."

At the end of Cream's US tour in June, Jack admitted something that would have been unimaginable before that titanic crossing through America: "I ran away to England," but, as he added right after, "they had to come and bring me back!"[9]

He was referring to Cream's farewell tour, which was called when the band realized they were at the seams and couldn't see a future down the road. This last tour ran from October 4, at Oakland Coliseum, to November 4, 1968, at Rhode Island Auditorium. The ballroom days were over; the touch between Cream and the audience that was still close at the Fillmore was progressively lost by the time the band started playing stadiums and arenas.

Cream gave their last bow on November 26 at the Royal Albert Hall, in England, the country that, not even two years before, the band had vowed never to look back to, and where now it was running back to.

Two years before, a conviction was running through the country that Cream wouldn't last, because each member was a superstar and their egos would collide irreversibly. In late 1968, that inauspicious foretelling proved true: Cream left England with the intent to be *one* and came back as three musicians drifting apart. Among all the other reasons, there were also Ginger's and Jack's temperamental behaviors and incompatible personalities that went at the seams, while Eric witnessed in horror.

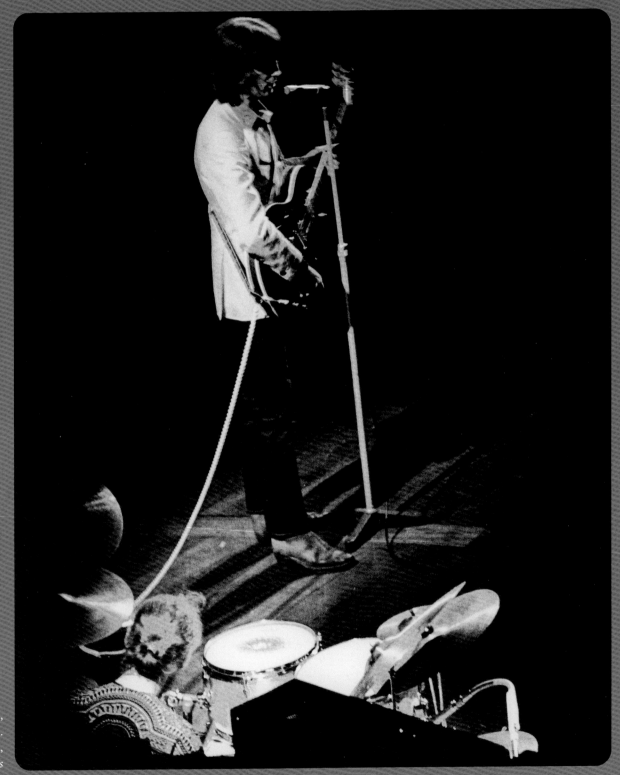

Cream Farewell Concert,
Royal Albert Hall, London.
Tuesday, November 26,
1968. *Photo by Chris Thomas*

"We had lost our direction," remembered Eric:

Our gigs had become nothing more than an excuse for us to show off as individuals, and any sense of unity that we might have had when we started out seemed to have gone out of the window. We also suffered from an inability to get on. We would just run away from one another. We never socialized together, we never really shared ideas any more. We just got together on stage and played and then went our separate ways.[10]

Jack Bruce returned to Glasgow, Scotland, where he started leading a solitary lifestyle with his family and began working on his first solo album, *Songs for a Tailor*, which would be released in 1969. Tony Palmer visited him and made a documentary on this new page of Cream's bass player, called *Rope Ladder to the Moon*.

Ginger Baker always attributed his hearing problems to the last 1968 tours with Cream, with amps' volumes reaching deafening levels.

Eric seemed the one who left Cream in the worst shape. He was described as out of his depth, almost in a serious dissociation with himself. As Chris Welch observed, "It took many years for Clapton to recover from the traumatic Cream experience. It had been so challenging musically, yet so physically and emotionally draining."

"The success of Cream left a huge scar," said Eric.[11]

Of all the reasons that contributed to Eric's detachment from Cream, there is one that affected him more than the rest: on May 11, 1968, *Rolling Stone* magazine published a poisonous article by Jon Landau that harshly wrote off the band and especially the guitarist, defining him, among all things, "a master of the blues clichés."[12] The *Rolling Stone* article "just soured things for Eric," said Jack Bruce, adding also that it was one of the main elements that made Cream lose their balance.[13]

It undoubtedly contributed to sharpening and intensifying the guitarist's solitary and reserved self, leading him to embrace a more intimate attitude to life and music.

This episode occurred almost simultaneously with the release of *Music from Big Pink* by former Bob Dylan sidemen the Band, in which Eric saw the reflection of the completely new frame of mind he was starting to mature.

With this perspective, Eric's longtime friend and Cream roadie Ben Palmer remembered, "He didn't want to work in that kind of atmosphere any more. By then, Eric sought the company of those people who[m] he could get along with the better and without all that tension."[14]

In all the confusion that arose from the hectic Cream experience, Eric had grown a new perspective on his role in a band; he momentarily abandoned the virtuoso frontman and solo guitarist outfit that Cream had stitched on him and decided he would have to become "one in the band," whatever band it may have been in the future.

Uncertain it may have been, Eric turned to his future with the only certainty he had since he first picked up the guitar: "I am and always will be a blues guitarist."[15]

At least for now, away from Cream, Eric finally found a way to live.

San Diego Sports Arena, San Diego, California. October 20, 1968.

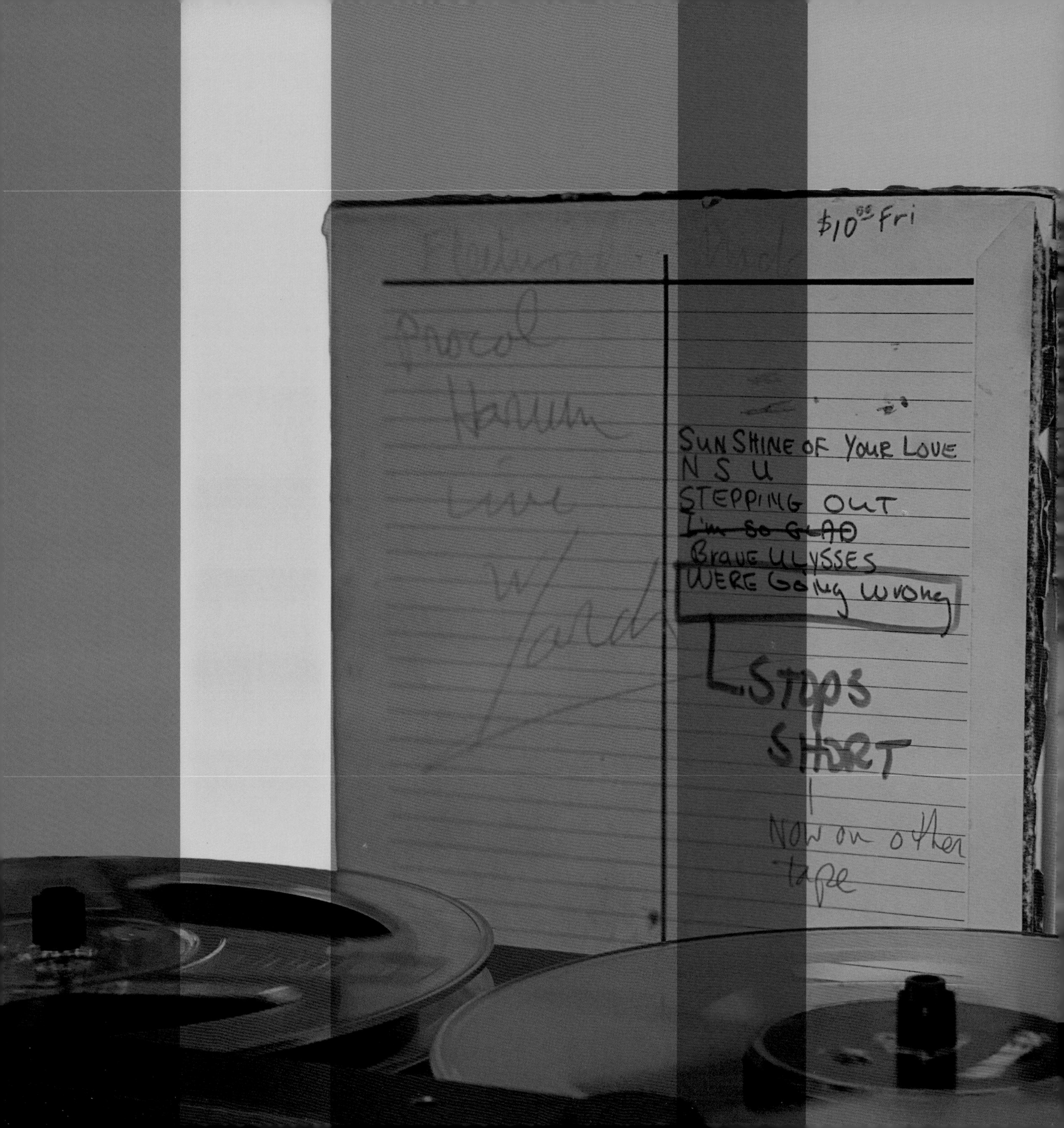

$10⁰⁰ Fri

Procol
Harum
Live
w/
Yard

SUNSHINE OF YOUR LOVE
N S U
STEPPING OUT
I'm so GLAD
BRAVE ULYSSES
WERE GOING WRONG

STOPS
SHORT
|
NOW on other
tape

Endnotes

Chapter 1

1. Eric Corder, "The Cream Rises," *G.Q. Scene*, Spring/Summer 1968, 78.
2. Pete Johnson, "Cream Guitarist, a Reluctant Idol," *Calendar*, *Los Angeles Times*, October 13, 1968, 1 and 37.
3. John Brewer, dir., Eric Clapton interview, in *Classic Artists: Cream*, Classic Artists (DVD Music Media, 2006).
4. Gregory McDonald, "The Cream," *Boston Sunday Globe*, June 16, 1968, 14–19.
5. Corder, "The Cream Rises."
6. McDonald, "The Cream."
7. Jim Delehant, "An Interview with Eric Clapton," *Hit Parader*, March 1968, 22–25.
8. Delehant, "An Interview with Eric Clapton."
9. Beat Instrumental, "Eric Answers Questions on the Clapton Way of Life," *Beat Instrumental*, August 1967.
10. Delehant, "An Interview with Eric Clapton."
11. Jim Delehant, "Making the Cream Work," *Hit Parader*, November 1968, 36–40.
12. Pete Brown, *Cream*, Classic Artists, 2006.
13. Chris Welch, *Cream* (London: Balafon Books, 2000), 101.

Chapter 2

1. Chris Welch, "Clapton: Back to the Blues," *Melody Maker*, May 4, 1968, 10–11.
2. Eric Clapton, *The Autobiography* (London: Arrow Books, 2008), 91–92.
3. Clapton, *The Autobiography*, 86.
4. Melody Maker, "A Frenzy of Whipped Cream in New York," *Melody Maker*, April 22, 1967, 7.
5. Bill Graham and Robert Greenfield, *Bill Graham Presents: My Life Inside Rock and Out* (Boston: Da Capo, 2004), 216–17.
6. Corder, "The Cream Rises."

7. Beat Instrumental, "Eric Answers Questions on the Clapton Way of Life."
8. Pop/Rock Music, "Hardly a Scream for Cream," *Pop/Rock Music*, December 1968, 44–45.
9. Joel Selvin, *The Haight: Love, Rock, and Revolution; The Photography of Jim Marshall*, rev. and expanded ed. (San Rafael, CA: Insight Editions, 2021), 39.
10. Graham and Greenfield, *Bill Graham Presents: My Life Inside Rock and Out*, 135.
11. Graham and Greenfield, *Bill Graham Presents: My Life Inside Rock and Out*: 124.
12. Selvin, *The Haight: Love, Rock, and Revolution*, 41.
13. Clapton, *The Autobiography*, 96.
14. Welch, *Cream*, 113.
15. Ibid.
16. Jon Landau, "The Rolling Stone Interview: Eric Clapton," *Rolling Stone*, May 11, 1968.
17. Light into Ashes, "Cream and the Dead," *Grateful Dead Guide* (blog), https://deadessays.blogspot.com.
18. Bob Dawbarn, "Super Cream Whip Up US Audiences," *Melody Maker*, October 28, 1967.

Chapter 3
1. Delehant, "An Interview with Eric Clapton."
2. Brewer, Eric Clapton interview, *Classic Artists: Cream*.
3. Paste Magazine, "Jim Marshall, Michael Zagaris, Baron Wolman Interview, 7/27/2006," https://www.youtube.com/watch?v=Ksl2MJ1Jr1E.

San Francisco, February 29–March 3
1. Tony Palmer, phone conversation with author, February 7, 2021.
2. Graham and Greenfield, *Bill Graham Presents: My Life Inside Rock and Out*, 214.
3. Jeff Godoy, Facebook message to author, September 18, 2021.
4. Tony Palmer, phone conversation with author, February 7, 2021.

5. Selvin, *The Haight: Love, Rock, and Revolution*, 300–303.
6. Tony Palmer, phone conversation with author, February 7, 2021.
7. Ibid.
8. Nick Schram, email message to author, October 28, 2021.
9. Graham and Greenfield, *Bill Graham Presents: My Life Inside Rock and Out*, 237.
10. Nick Schram, email message to author, October 28, 2021.
11. Ibid.

San Francisco, March 7–10
1. Chris Wilson, dir., *The Art of Drumming* (Sky Arts, 2018).
2. Clapton, *The Autobiography*, 100.
3. Welch, *Cream*, 123.
4. Jody Rosen, "The Day the Music Burned," *New York Times*, June 11, 2019.
5. Larry Yelen, email message to author, October 22, 2021.
6. Larry Yelen through Michael Chaiken, email message to author, June 9, 2019.
7. Nick Schram, email message to author, June 18, 2021.

Chapter 4
1. Welch, *Cream*, 120.
2. Welch, "Clapton: Back to the Blues."
3. Clapton, *The Autobiography*, 100.
4. Welch, *Cream*, 156.
5. Clapton, *The Autobiography*, 80.
6. Welch, "Clapton: Back to the Blues."
7. Welch, *Cream*, 101.
8. Welch, "Clapton: Back to the Blues."
9. Ralph J. Gleason, "The Cream Has Been Whipped," *San Francisco Examiner*, October 13, 1968.
10. Clapton, *The Autobiography*, 103.
11. Welch, *Cream*, 157.
12. Jon Landau, "Cream," *Rolling Stone*, May 11, 1968.
13. Welch, *Cream*, 140.
14. Ibid., 139.
15. Welch, "Clapton: Back to the Blues."

Bibliography

Adorno, Theodor W. *Negative Dialectics*. London: Routledge, 1990.

Baker, Ginger. *Hellraiser: The Autobiography of the World's Greatest Drummer*. London: John Blake, 2010.

Beat Instrumental. "Eric Answers Questions on the Clapton Way of Life." *Beat Instrumental*, August 1967.

Brewer, Jon, dir. *Classic Artists: Cream*. Classic Artists. DVD Music Media, 2006.

Bulger, Jay. *Beware of Mr. Baker*. DVD. New York: SnagFilms, 2012.

Chaiken, Michael. *Pop: Ancient and Modern*. In *The Complete Monterey Pop Festival*. Directed by D. A. Pennebaker. Blu-Ray. New York: Criterion Collection, 2017.

Clapton, Eric. *The Autobiography*. London: Arrow Books, 2008.

Corder, Eric. "The Cream Rises." *G.Q. Scene*, Spring/Summer 1968.

Dawbarn, Bob. "Super Cream Whip Up US Audiences." *Melody Maker*, October 28, 1967.

Delehant, Jim. "An Interview with Eric Clapton." *Hit Parader*, March 1968.

———. "Making the Cream Work." *Hit Parader*, November 1968.

Genzolini, Edoardo. *The Who: Concert Memories from the Classic Years, 1964–1976*. Atglen, PA: Schiffer, 2022.

Gleason, Ralph J. "The Cream Has Been Whipped." *San Francisco Examiner*, October 13, 1968.

———. *Jefferson Airplane and the San Francisco Sound*. New York: Ballantine Books, 1969.

Graham, Bill, and Robert Greenfield. *Bill Graham Presents: My Life Inside Rock and Out*. Boston: Da Capo, 2004.

Henri, Robert. "The New York Exhibition of Independent Artists." *The Craftsman* 18, no. 2 (May 1910).

Johnson, Pete. "Cream Guitarist, a Reluctant Idol." *Calendar, Los Angeles Times*, October 13, 1968.

Landau, Jon. "The Rolling Stone Interview: Eric Clapton." *Rolling Stone*, May 11, 1968.

Larsen, Christian. *Clapton Live History*. Aarhus, Denmark: C. Larsen & Sons, 2019.

Light into Ashes. *Grateful Dead Guide* (blog). https://deadessays.blogspot.com.

McDonald, Gregory. "The Cream." *Boston Sunday Globe*, June 16, 1968.

McGee, Rosie. *Dancing with the Dead: A Photographic Memoir; My Good Old Days with the Grateful Dead & the San Francisco Music Scene, 1964–1974*. Rohnert Park, CA: Tioli Press & Bytes, 2013.

Melody Maker. "A Frenzy of Whipped Cream in New York." *Melody Maker*, April 22, 1967.

Nizan, Paul. *Aden, Arabie*. University Park: Pennsylvania State University Press, 1970.

Pop/Rock Music. "Hardly a Scream for Cream." *Pop/Rock Music*, December 1968.

Roberty, Marc. *Eric Clapton: Day by Day*. Vol. 1, *The Early Years, 1963–1982*. London: Backbeat Books, 2013.

Rosen, Jody. "The Day the Music Burned." *New York Times*, June 11, 2019.

Schlegel, Friedrich. *Dialogue on Poetry and Literary Aphorisms*. University Park: Pennsylvania State University Press, 1990.

Selvin, Joel. *Altamont: The Rolling Stones, the Hells Angels, and the Inside Story of Rock's Darkest Day*. New York: Dey Street Books, 2016.

———. *The Haight: Love, Rock, and Revolution; The Photography of Jim Marshall*. Rev. and expanded ed. San Rafael, CA: Insight Editions, 2021.

———. *Summer of Love: The Inside Story of LSD, Rock & Roll, Free Love & High Times in the Wild West*. New York: E. P. Dutton, 1994.

Shapiro, Harry. *Jack Bruce Composing Himself: The Authorized Biography*. London: Jawbone, 2010.

Welch, Chris. "Clapton: Back to the Blues." *Melody Maker*, May 4, 1968.

———. *Cream*. London: Balafon Books, 2000.

Wilson, Chris, dir. *The Art of Drumming: Ginger Baker*. Sky Arts, 2018.

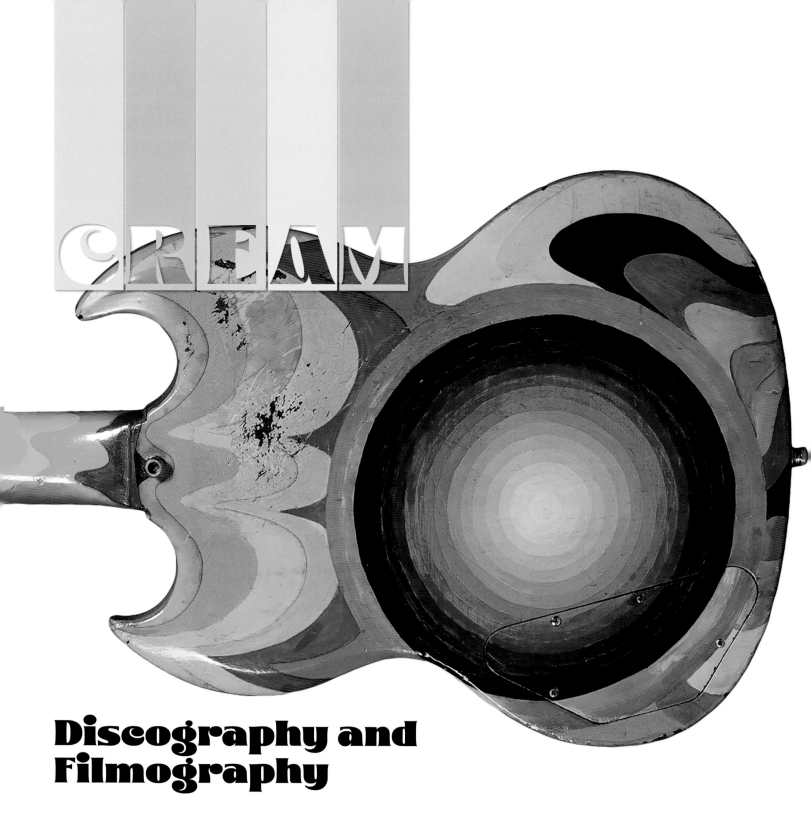

CREAM

Discography and Filmography

Studio albums

Fresh Cream (UK: December 9, 1966, Reaction 593/4 001, mono/stereo—US: January 1967, ATCO 33-206 / SD 33-206, mono/stereo)

Disraeli Gears (UK: November 2, 1967, Reaction 593/4 003, mono/stereo—US: November 2, 1967, ATCO 33-232 / SD 33-232, mono/stereo)

Wheels of Fire [studio/live] (UK: August 9, 1968, Polydor 582/3 031/2, mono/stereo—US: June 14, 1968, ATCO SD 2-700, mono/stereo)

Goodbye [studio/live] (UK: February 5, 1969, Polydor 593 053, stereo—US: February 5, 1969, ATCO SD 7001, stereo)

Live albums

Live Cream (UK: April 1970, Polydor 2383 016, stereo—US: April 1970, ATCO SD 33-328, stereo)

Live Cream Volume II (UK: March 2, 1972, Polydor 2383 119, stereo—US: March 2, 1972, ATCO SD 7005, stereo)

BBC Sessions (March 25, 2003, Polydor LC 00309.076048-2)

Royal Albert Hall, London, May 2–3–5–6, 2005 (October 4, 2005, Reprise 9362-49416-2)

Compilation albums

Best of Cream (UK: October 24, 1969, Polydor 583 060, stereo—US: October 24, 1969, ATCO SD 33-291, stereo)

Heavy Cream (UK: October 9, 1972, Polydor 2659 022, stereo—US: October 9, 1972, Polydor PD-3502)

Cream Off the Top (April 1973, Polydor PD 5529, stereo)

Strange Brew: The Very Best of Cream (UK: 1983, RSO Deluxe [RSO 5021], stereo—US: 1983, RSO 811639, stereo)

The Very Best of Cream (May 9, 1995, Polydor/Chronicles 523752-2)

Those Were the Days (September 23, 1997, Polydor 539000-2)

20th Century Masters: The Millennium Collection—The Best of Cream (February 29, 2000, Polydor 543498)

Cream—Gold (April 25, 2005, Polydor 4193)

I Feel Free—Ultimate Cream (May 31, 2005, Polydor 987136)

Icon (June 21, 2011, Polydor B004ZQBP54)

The Alternative Album (April 8, 2013, Itm B00A9V1R02)

The Origins (September 12, 2018, Vintage Jukebox)

Goodbye Tour—Live 1968 (March 6, 2020, Polydor B07ZWBMD3D)

Unofficial live recordings

Klook's Kleek, London, UK. November 15, 1966 (00:31:45)

Konserthusert, Stockholm, Sweden. March 7, 1967 (00:26:28)

Ricky Tick, Hounslow, West London, UK. April 22, 1967 (00:40:55)

Barbecue '67, Spalding, Lincolnshire, UK. May 29, 1967 (00:40:17)

Fillmore Auditorium, San Francisco, CA. September 3, 1967 (01:05:40)

Brandeis University, Waltham , MA. September 9, 1967 (01:21:12)

Psychedelic Supermarket, Boston, MA. September 10–16, 1967 (00:30:58)

Village Theater, New York. September 23, 1967 (00:07:17)

Grande Ballroom, Detroit, MI. October 15, 1967 (01:48:52)

Konserthusert, Stockholm, Sweden. November 14, 1967 (01:06:37)

Santa Monica Civic, Santa Monica, CA. February 23, 1968 (00:09:49)

Fillmore Auditorium, San Francisco, CA. March 3, 1968 (01:22:00)

Fillmore Auditorium, San Francisco, CA. March 3, 1968, by Nick Schram (00:46:37)

Winterland, San Francisco, CA. March 9, 1968, by Mark d'Ercole (00:54:42)

Fillmore Auditorium, San Francisco, CA. March 10, 1968 (01:17:41)

Fillmore Auditorium, San Francisco, CA. March 10, 1968, by Nick Schram/George Chacona (00:51:71)

Shapiro Athletic Center, Brandeis University, Waltham (MA). March 23, 1968 (01:24:20)

State Fair Music Hall, Dallas, TX. March 30, 1968 (00:56:41)

Back Bay Theater, Boston, MA. April 5, 1968 (01:22:25)

Civic Auditorium, San Jose, CA. May 25, 1968 (01:03:17)

Saule Arena, Montreal, Canada. June 11, 1968 (01:05:40)

Oakdale Music Center, Wallingford, CN. June 15, 1968 (01:07:33)

University of New Mexico, Albuquerque, NM. October 5, 1968 (01:05:10)

Denver Auditorium Arena, Denver, CO. October 6, 1968 (00:57:58)

Civic Opera House, Chicago, IL. October 7, 1968 (01:15:53)

New Haven Arena, New Haven, CT. October 11, 1968 (01:04:56, 01:07:13)

Olympia Stadium, Detroit, MI. October 12, 1968 (00:11:13)

Chicago Coliseum, Chicago, IL. October 13, 1968 (01:00:45)

Memorial Auditorium, Dallas, TX. October 25, 1968 (01:22:54)

Madison Square Garden, New York. November 2, 1968 (01:19:02, 01:12:25, 00:59:12)

Rhode Island Auditorium, Providence, RI. November 4, 1968 (00:36:29)

Singles

"Wrapping Paper" / "Cat's Squirrel" (1966)

"I Feel Free" / "N.S.U." (1966)

"Strange Brew" / "Tales of Brave Ulysses" (1967)

"Spoonful" (part one) / "Spoonful" (part two) (1967)

"Sunshine of Your Love" / "SWLABR" (1968)

"Anyone for Tennis" / "Pressed Rat and Warthog" (1968)

"White Room" / "Those Were the Days" (1968)

"Crossroads" / "Passing the Time" (1969)

"Badge" / "What a Bringdown" (1969)

"Lawdy Mama" / "Sweet Wine" (1970)

Essential film appearances

Les Cream au Revolution Club (dir. Jean Paul Thomas)—Cream filmed by French television at the Revolution Club in Mayfair, London, on January 10, 1968.

All My Loving (dir. Tony Palmer)—Cream filmed at Winterland (San Francisco, CA) on March 2 and March 9, 1968, and on *Twice a Fortnight* at the BBC around November 1967. *All My Loving* was first broadcasted on BBC1 on Sunday, November 3, 1968, at 10:40 p.m.

Det var en lørdag aften (dir. Erik Balling, 1968). Cream mime "World of Pain" in a cold day in Copenhagen, Denmark.

Farewell Concert from the Royal Albert Hall, London (dir. Tony Palmer). Filmed on November 26, 1968, and broadcasted by the BBC on January 5, 1969.

Fresh Live Cream (dir. Martin Baker). Interviews and previously unreleased material after the band's 1993 Rock and Roll Hall of Fame induction.

Royal Albert Hall, May 2–3–5–6, 2005 (dir. J. V. Walther, M. Atkins).

Cream: Disraeli Gears (*Classic Albums* series, 2006)—the making of Cream's classic album.

Cream (Classic Artists series. Dir. Jon Brewer, 2006)—interviews before and after the October 24–26, 2005, reunion concerts at Madison Square Garden. It also features an audio CD with tracks recorded from Swedish radio at Konserthusert in Stockholm, Sweden, on March 7, 1967.

Original transparency of one of Nick Schram's photos from the Fillmore, March 7, 1968.

This Weekend at Bill Gr

T

(B

THURSDAY & S

FILLMO

FRIDAY & SAT

POST

JEREMY &
THE SATYRS
$2.99

2309 TELEGRAPH AVENUE
BERKELEY • 849-3332
MON-FRI 9:30 to 10 • SAT 9:30-6
SUN. 12-5